We Are the ARK

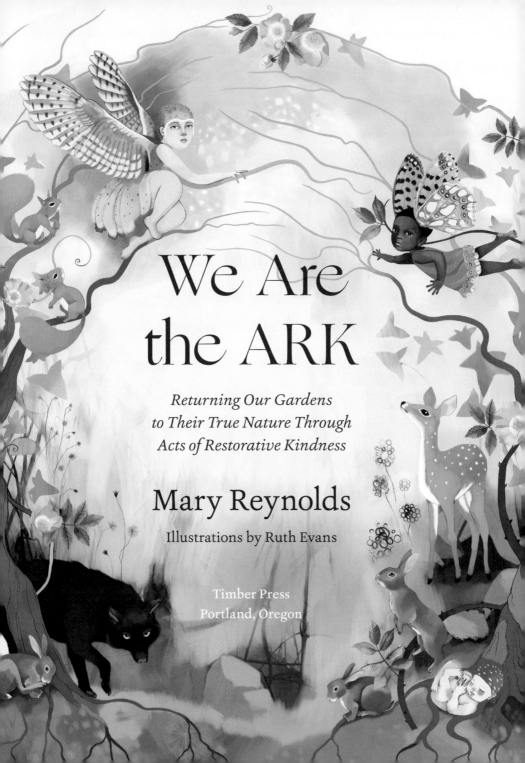

We Are the ARK

*Returning Our Gardens
to Their True Nature Through
Acts of Restorative Kindness*

Mary Reynolds

Illustrations by Ruth Evans

Timber Press
Portland, Oregon

Published in 2022 by Timber Press, Inc.

The Haseltine Building
133 S.W. Second Avenue, Suite 450
Portland, Oregon 97204-3527
timberpress.com

Printed in China on paper
from responsible sources

Text design by Faceout Studio, Paul Nielsen
Jacket design by Vincent James
Cover illustration by Ruth Evans

ISBN 978-1-64326-178-2

Catalog records for this book are available
from the Library of Congress and the
British Library.

This book is dedicated
to my mother Earth, my true
family, the rooted and unrooted, the
seen and unseen. Thank you for affording
me the gift of life on this beautiful shared
home of ours.

My life is yours.

Your health is mine.

This book, this movement,
this work, is all for you.

Contents

Preface: What This Book Is About

A few years ago, my increasing awareness of the collapse in biodiversity and the lack of safe space for wildlife led me to start a movement called We Are the ARK. I ask people to give at least half of any land under their care back to nature and to grow their own food in the other half if possible. The time has come for humans to step up and share this earth, which we are impossibly lucky to inhabit, with the countless other creatures who also call it home, beginning with our own patches of it.

We need to start considering that gardens are part of an old world and to adopt a new vision for our future. Our relationship with nature must change. Looking at gardens as artistic endeavours or feasts for our senses is outmoded. ARKs are gardens that we have released from bondage. ARK building is focused on restoring native ecosystems and adding extra creature supports, to provide space and sanctuary for our shared kin, the rooted and unrooted.

The chapters ahead focus specifically on the parts of your garden that you are turning into an ARK. If you have already turned all your land into a vegetable garden or a food forest, filled with edible and medicinal plants, that is perfectly fine; stepping outside the food system is a big part of ARKing. But there are probably still places you can put native plants and other creature supports, and all good intentions are welcomed and appreciated by our wild kin.

May it fill your heart with joy to extend your family to include every insect, native plant or animal, and fluffy bird that finds sanctuary there with you.

THIS IS AN ARK ♥

ARKs and the Great Remembering

An ARK is a restored native ecosystem—a local small, medium, or large rewilding project. It is an Act of Restorative Kindness to the earth, a thriving patch of native plants and creatures that have been supported to reestablish in the earth's intelligent successional processes of natural restoration. Over time this becomes a pantry and a habitat for our pollinators and wild creatures of every kind, who are in desperate need of support.

This takes a while to happen, but with our help a simple ecosystem begins to reappear very quickly. Over time, with some planning and additional supports if necessary, it grows into a healthy wildlife habitat and eventually a multitiered, complex community of native plants, creatures, and microorganisms. It becomes a source of seeds of restoration for an increasingly barren earth.

You need no money to create an ARK, just the will to be part of the solution, to be kind and caring. Not all of us are lucky enough to have a patch of the planet under our care, but you can do so much to raise awareness in other ways, through community activities and creating ARKs on public lands or at your local schools and parks. Even a window box can be a wonderful mini ARK.

We Are the ARK is a grassroots movement that has spread all around the world, trying to restore as many individual patches of earth as possible. It's a movement owned by all of us who care about the earth. The secret ARK world domination plan aims to give so many pieces of this earth back to nature that we can eventually join it all up in a big patchwork quilt of hope for our future that will wrap its way around the globe.

Birth of We Are the ARK

It wasn't the startled fox that grabbed my attention from the drawing board where I was daydreaming out the window at home. It was the pair of hares that were chasing the fox across the garden. Soon afterward, I spotted a hedgehog scurrying along the hares' path but well tucked under the protection of the thick hawthorn hedge that edged the lawn in front of me. They all disappeared into the wildness that was one half of the land I was minding, taking refuge in an acre of self-willed land—a mix of thorny shrubs, brambles, grasses, and rushes to the west of my garden.

Seeing as it was early winter and a bright mid-morning, I figured something must be amiss for the normally hidden, feral creatures to cross my path in such a manner, so I got up from my work and went outside to investigate. I followed the direction they were coming from and wandered up to the end of my laneway, onto the quiet country road where I live in Ireland.

Not so quiet today, however.

Across the road, there used to be an acre of thick, impenetrable, self-willed land that had grown dense with prickly gorse, thorny brambles, spiky hawthorn and blackthorn, and voracious bracken. Today, a big yellow monster of destruction had landed. My neighbours had finally gotten planning permission to build a house, so they did what everyone does: they sent in a digger to clear out "the mess" and make a garden, without any thought for the multiple families who already called it home.

I stood there in absolute horror, forgetting to breathe. I had done this myself so many times, in so many places. For more than twenty years I had been working all over the world as a garden designer, carrying out similar unconscious devastation everywhere I worked.

It was suddenly blindingly obvious to me that these creatures we are supposed to share our earth with have fewer and fewer safe places left to go. Agricultural land is soaked in vast quantities of increasingly potent chemicals that make it impossible for wildlife to survive, and their habitats and foraging places are being torn out at a rapid rate to ensure desperate farmers can utilize every last square foot of land. There is no sanctuary for them in our gardens, which we fill with purchased, pretty, non-native "garden plants." Gardens are controlled and poisoned to the point of being a still life, with no room at the inn for anything other than our own visions of how we want things to be.

I went back inside and started researching the collapse of the natural world, learning very quickly that the biodiversity crisis is even more insidious and dangerous than the looming threat of climate collapse because it is not understood or given much attention. *Biodiversity* is short for *biological diversity*. *Biodiversity* is defined as the variety of all living things, and the systems that connect them. This includes all the planet's different plants, animals, and microorganisms, plus the genetic information they contain and the ecosystems of which they are a part. Extraordinarily, the devastating decline of biodiversity is happening at an incredible speed, mostly within the last fifty years, coinciding with the rapid acceleration of chemical farming, industrial forestry, and destructive overfishing.

The web of life is being pushed to the edge, and we are unquestionably and indivisibly (if often unknowingly) tethered to that web. All creatures play a vital role in the circle of life. When a gap appears in that circle or a strand of that web disappears, the system gets weaker and closer to collapse. We rely upon every creature's presence for our clean air and water, healthy foods, and beautiful environments. What's not so obvious is how many of these species form the basis of the earth's immune system— and indeed, our own continued protection from disease. Each moment of our lives is dependent on this web of life remaining intact.

Multiple species are now falling prey to extinction every single day. They are never coming back.

This is the great forgetting.

Almost nothing is being done to halt this decline because the industrial farming, fishing, forestry, and gardening industries are either downright ignorant or simply unable to stop their self-catapulted ride over the edge of the cliff.

Knowing I couldn't take on the whole world, I tried not to get overwhelmed and instead put the kettle on and sat down at my kitchen table to think about what one person could do that would really make a difference to our current trajectory.

All the greatest changes in history have come from the ground up—from small movements of passionate and focused people. Everything must change, and I saw clearly that we couldn't wait for political solutions anymore. We all needed to step up and become the leaders. So after the second cup of tea that day, I came up with a plan. I decided I could tackle my industry of choice: the world of gardening.

I had an idea to begin a grassroots movement called We Are the ARK (for Acts of Restorative Kindness to the earth), a simple concept that asks people to give as much land back to nature as they can spare. I decided to restore my own patch of earth, my garden, back to its true nature and to inspire others to do the same, to make a difference person by person. To build ARKs for our shared kin, rooted and unrooted.

The following February, I worked with my friends Claire and Joe from the Irish Forest Garden, Ruth Evans the artist, and Jenn Halter-Prenda, our web designer friend, to put together a simple homemade website to support this idea—a resource to help people understand why we need ARKs, how to turn their garden into an ARK, and how they can add more creature support systems depending on their abilities and situations.

I am a big supporter of E. O. Wilson's Half-Earth Project, which proposes that we give half of the earth back to our wild kin (including the Indigenous peoples), to return it to its true nature. In that spirit, I am asking people who are are lucky enough to have some land under their care to consider setting at least half of it free and supporting it to become as useful a sanctuary as possible to the local flora and fauna. I suggest that if they can't manage to ARK half of their land, then any they can spare, even if it's just the boundaries, is welcome and important. Finally, I also propose stepping out of the destructive food system if possible and trying to grow as much of their own organic food as they can in the other half.

I am asking people to share the earth, patch by patch.

Within months of launching the idea, I had thousands of "ARKevists" all around the world, all active members of an online group I set up. Luckily, I found a bunch of wonderful members to help me run it with kindness— namely Moya McGinley, Fran Mills, Sèan Bergin, and Clare Meleady Smith. Some ARKs are as big as 1,500 acres in the United States; some are as small as a window box in Norway. Members are constantly sharing stories and photos of all sorts of marvellous creatures that make homes in their ARK sanctuaries. Every day new members are added and new plots of land restored to nature.

The key to the success of the movement is the home-made signs proudly displayed in every ARK stating, "This is an ARK," with our website address included for reference. These signs explain away the inherent cultural shame of a messy garden or landscape and instead mark out the owner as a proud part of a new and kinder world, a world where we are embracing our roles as caretakers of the earth and of as many creatures as our ARKs can sustain.

The wonderful side effect, which I had not envisaged, is that people are finding hope in their ARKs. When they create their sanctuaries, they feel as if their families have expanded to include each native mammal, insect, bird, fungus, and wild weed that comes to stay. People are suddenly looking over the neighbours' fences and seeing the wasted opportunities that gardens are now revealed to them to be. As almost still-life expressions of people's creativity, gardens are beginning to look more and more pointless and needlessly selfish to those of us who have rediscovered nature's true beauty. Green spaces on university campuses, school grounds, and industrial estates are suddenly obvious places for ARKs. People are putting up signs (with permission) saying "This could be an ARK!"

This is something real. The results have been so fast in arriving and so inspiring and empowering for people, it goes way beyond the satisfaction of changing their lightbulbs or getting a reusable cup for their daily coffee (though every little action helps!).

Everything has changed for all of us budding ARK protectors, and a global movement has begun.

The Garden Industry and the Great Forgetting

A long, long time ago, when the earth had a full set of clothes and our ancestors were subject to the ravages of nature, an understandable movement began in many cultures to create enclosures for protection, control, and safety. Gardens were born. Initially, these little corrals made sense, but gradually they began to separate humans from each other and all other life forms.

The history of landscape design is a record of the multiple cultural guillotines that severed us from nature. It illustrates our slow slide from grace. From purposeful guardians of the earth without boundaries or ownership, humans became plant artistes, garden designers, landscape architects, earth sculptors, and statement makers, working and designing with living sentient beings as our canvas and materials of choice.

Most gardens are green deserts for our shared kin, at least relative to wild places. Creativity is a vital part of human life, but we have got to learn how to be creative without causing damage to nature.

It's time to learn to share.

Everything we are made of comes from the earth and her atmosphere. This earth body is like a huge nourishing heart. When we began to look at the earth in terms of ownership rather than guardianship, that heart smashed into millions of tiny pieces. It is still breaking. But now our job is to give her hope, to heal her heart. We are here for only a moment in time, so the idea of ownership of the eternal earth is a bit odd. Still, each plot of land is "owned" by somebody, and piece by piece we can set it free and give it back to her, removing the walls between. We can help her grow her clothes back, allow her the space to look after all her creatures, the seen and unseen.

Nature abhors a vacuum, and she will strive to mend any cuts in her skin with her natural healing processes, beginning with the weeds. The earth is very resilient, but sometimes these days, she needs our help with this process of restoring her natural layers so that all the spaces are filled in and the unrooted creatures can find food and shelter once more. There is also a rising need for resting places where nature can develop the mechanisms to digest, counteract, and disassemble the toxins we have soaked her with.

We need a wave of change, a tumultuous shift of intention for the industry of gardening. But like almost every other destructive modern industry, it exists only if we support it. If we step off that treadmill and turn our gardens into ARKs, the industry will either suffer or become an ARK supporter, because, like any other industry, it is ultimately about profit, and we have the muscle to force change through our spending power. The industry will follow the money.

Unfortunately, the gardening industry has gotten away with those damaging consequences for a long time, as there is a false belief that gardening is a green activity, a way to connect with and be in nature. But most gardens are no longer nature friendly. They are filled with non-native plants that have not evolved within the local food web and are not supportive of life and its intricate relationships. The choice of plants to dress up these "outdoor rooms" is driven by subtle marketing and fashionable makeover programmes that dictate and direct the general public's concept of beauty.

Garden centres and nurseries are among the largest sellers of chemicals and pesticides. Gardens now typically use ten times more chemicals by volume per acre than industrially farmed agricultural land. These chemicals are all potent poisons to nature and the whole web of life, including ourselves.

Peatlands, a type of wetland that occurs in almost every part of the world, account for just 3 percent of the world's landmass but store twice as much carbon as all of the world's forests combined. Our precious peatlands are mined to serve gardening needs. This is akin to bulldozing the rainforests, which most good people would be horrified to be consciously part of. Demand your local nurseries stock organic native plants grown in peat-free substrates. Your pocketbook drives the change.

The growth of landscaping plants in peat-based compost in heated glasshouses ensures a carbon-heavy beginning. Their consequent exportation to foreign lands to go on sale to the public from nurseries and garden centres has caused the spread of many terrible diseases for plants and wildlife.

As colonization occurred across the world, ousting the Indigenous peoples, the settlers brought plants for food and medicine with them. Many of these plants have naturalized, so it really does take a concerted effort to recognize native versus non-native species. Many invasive plants have also "escaped" from gardens. The fallout is catastrophic. Invasive plants are running rampant in ecosystems they did not evolve alongside, with no checks to maintain them as part of a balanced web. Their impact on the local food web is devastating for the native creatures.

And that's just the beginning. Even the wildlife gardening narrative often focuses on supporting the industry rather than offering the truth of what wildlife really needs to survive.

THE FLAWED WILDLIFE GARDENING NARRATIVE

In many ways, our crazy history of importing non-native plants into our gardens has done so much damage. Traditional wildlife gardening would have you plant a selection of "bird and butterfly" plants. In Ireland I see garden centres promoting lavenders and buddleia (butterfly bush), for example—and yes, it's true that bees and butterflies love them. Some of the introduced garden plants that are promoted as wildlife supports are very attractive to many pollinators. It is usually their showy blooms that grab pollinators' attention, along with the attention of the gardeners who are made to feel they are doing great work by planting such things in their gardens.

However, these showy flowers can monopolize the attention of pollinators. Sadly, this leads to pollinators paying less attention to native flowering plants, and this greatly reduces the ability of many plants to set seed successfully. This leads to degradation of the local ecosystem as insects cannot find their native plant partners, which means they cannot create a new generation of their species. Native plants are losing ground at a rapid rate.

I'm sure the gardening industry didn't mean to become so damaging, as it is filled with wonderful people with good hearts. But the industry is clearly causing serious problems for wildlife, rooted and unrooted. Even so, the blinkers are firmly on and change is resisted. Chemicals are used widely, with a sense of resignation and inevitability, and "low-maintenance gardening" has become the standard outcome to reach for in our landscapes.

The ARK concept challenges a whole group of people who depend upon the industry of gardening. I am aware that this is difficult, but the collapse of our natural world is a lot more intractable. The only options left to us are to change or to die, and we can't tiptoe around anymore. We are at the tail end of an emergency, a rapid collapse of nature's life support systems, and our very survival as a species is at risk.

We are quickly and silently running out of time, and everything has got to change. We have got to change.

Yes, change is hard and seems to happen only after disaster strikes. Luckily, people in the world of gardening have many opportunities available to them to become supporters of life within the work they do, to shift their focus and intention.

The core issue is this: we only get to live here in this incredibly beautiful, magical world if we understand that the health of the earth and every single one of her weird and wonderful creatures is now the most important consideration. Of all the millions of life forms that live here on this earth, we are the only ones with no obvious modern thread of connection to the web of life.

We have simply forgotten who we are.

Guardians, Not Gardeners

Now we must step into a vital role, by becoming the caretakers of the earth and all the magical beings we share her bounty with. By doing so we will find our true selves again in service to nature. It's the simplest thing imaginable, as easy or challenging as you choose, and can cost absolutely nothing. Gardens, on the other hand, cost us and the earth a lot.

The time for gardens as disconnected creative expressions has come to an end. Those gardens are mementos of the old world, and we need to build a new simple and kind world as quickly as possible. We do not need our garden enclosures to protect us from the wilderness anymore; we need to turn right around and embrace it. The wild creatures need as much space as possible to survive and we need them to be safe, to be well, to thrive, so that we may live. They need us to build them as many ARKs as possible, until we weave a web of connected sanctuaries that wrap their way around this planet and reboot the truth of who we are. Our ARKs will empower an army of warriors to protect and champion wild nature. These will be an important part of the seeds of nature's restoration when the time comes, when the new world has finally emerged from this dark time. They will be havens for life until it is safe to roam wide and free once more.

My dream is that the concept of treating your patch of this planet as an outdoor room will become a thing of the past, and that all of us who are awake and aware of the crisis we are in will turn at least some of our gardens into ARKs, creating a wave of change and empowerment that will quickly build into a roaring tsunami of life. There is so much joy, hope, satisfaction, and belonging available in restoring land to its truth, to its wild ways. Such wonder and beauty are on offer when we give our land back to nature, when we set it free. Once your eyes are opened, there is no going back to being a gardener. You will never look at your land the same way again. Once its true nature has been revealed, you will fall in love with it, because the earth's nature is truly magical and beautiful.

As is ours.

The act of building as many ARKs as possible and creating a patchwork quilt of healed earth, wrapping its way around the globe, will undoubtedly create a shift of consciousness in our relationship with the earth.

This is the great remembering.

We are here to be of service to the earth and all her creatures.

We are here to be guardians.

Not gardeners.

The Science
Bit and
ARKing Aims

As we make the transition from gardener to guardian, we must first realize that despite all the scientific knowledge available to us, we really know and understand very little about our earth. We live on a planet with a highly intelligent system of checks and balances.

Earth is a living organism, made up of millions of species all working together in harmonious and often mysterious ways. These are the threads of life. They support each other, control each other, and nourish each other. Each thread that we remove in our efforts to continue to grow exponentially and greedily expand our interests has a knock-on effect on the rest of the web.

We do not know when we will remove a thread that is holding it all together. We may already have done that. The tipping points may well have tipped already. We only get to live here on this magical, abundant paradise that we call Earth if the planet can continue to support us with clean air, water, and food.

Lingering without reason in my heart, there is still hope. Having worked with land for as long as I have, one thing I know is that nature recovers quickly; she has such strong resilience. All it takes is for us to set her free to restore her systems of life and to protect and support her while she recovers.

Our Shifting Baseline

Every generation has less and less awareness of what a truly healthy living landscape should look like. All over the world, within a couple of generations we have forgotten how abundant and alive the earth, her seas, and her skies used to be. We are dealing with an almost barren planet, but this is the new "natural" to younger generations.

Most of us have no memory of how crystal clear the seas used to be, kept that way by the lost ocean ecosystems of the rooted and unrooted, including the sea's natural filters, massive beds of oysters on the sea floor. We have forgotten how forests of kelp, seagrass, and seaweed lined the shallow waters of the coasts and how the waves were literally hopping with life. We don't remember what it was like to have shoals of fish in the rivers, to have oodles of birds, insects, frogs, butterflies, and hedgehogs sharing our world. There's very little living recollection left of how the skies would go dark momentarily when great swathes of butterflies or flocks of birds would block out the sun as they passed overhead in one of their heroic migratory journeys.

Children have no experience of what mature, native, natural woodlands look like. Only fragments of these multilayered living systems remain, and the concept of woodlands has been replaced with fast-growing non-native tree plantations. Monoculture forests are sown for profit and treated with vast quantities of chemicals, becoming dark deserts devoid of the diversity of life that normally lives in synchronicity and symbiosis with native woodland ecosystems.

When you're driving at night your windscreen is no longer covered in dead insects and moths like it used to be when you were a small child. Insect populations have plummeted. It is so quiet out there now, eerily quiet. We have reached Rachel Carson's predicted silent spring. Now there are only tiny wild pockets clinging on desperately, hoping for the two-legged ones to wake up and remember.

Our Irish hills are bare and green, overgrazed and kept that way by poorly managed sheep and deer and the absence of our native wolves. Those green hills have ironically become iconic images of these islands, which in fact exposes the hidden truth of nature here. Nature has already collapsed. It has mostly become a green desert, a sad state of affairs reflected in many parts of the world. Like the proverbial frog, unaware of the water heating in the pot he was sitting in, we have not noticed the changes.

As a species, we immediately forget what is lost and see only what exists right here, right now. Every generation is experiencing huge shifts in what passes for a natural system. These changes have become more extreme over the last few generations. What adults see as almost dead landscapes, our kids will perceive as natural and normal. There is a phrase for this phenomenon that most of us suffer from these days: *shifting baseline syndrome.* The term was first coined by marine biologist Daniel Pauly, who used it to describe scientists' baselines for healthy fish populations.

Professor of conservation science Dr. E. J. Milner-Gulland wrote in a paper about shifting baselines: "Generational amnesia is when knowledge is not passed down from generation to generation. For example, people may think of as 'pristine' wilderness the wild places that they experienced during their childhood, but with every generation this baseline becomes more and more degraded."

Three Basic Laws of Ecology

Paul Watson of the Sea Shepherd Conservation Society wrote down three basic laws of ecology that no living thing can survive outside of: the law of diversity, the law of interdependence, and the law of finite resources. I include his breakdown of Earth's ecological laws here as they made things simple and understandable for me. I hope their common sense strikes you, too, as I try to explain them as simply as possible.

The law of diversity states that the strength of an ecosystem depends upon the diversity of the species within it. We need the whole intricate web of life to be present to keep an ecosystem resilient and strong. The more diversity that is present, the stronger the ecosystem is. This is most easily seen in the consequences of the modern absence of apex predators in any ecosystem. Restore the predators and you restore the ecosystem. One famous example of this is the reintroduction of wolves in Yellowstone National Park in the United States starting in 1995.

Four years after their reintroduction, the wolves had directly caused the ecosystem to come back into balance and thrive once again. Without the presence of these apex predators, the elk and deer had run rampant through the park. They had overgrazed the plant ecosystems, which could not recover fast enough to support a stable, diverse community of interdependent life forms. This had had a hugely detrimental effect on the plant communities and their connected partners, rooted and unrooted. The trees had not been able to regenerate, and the berry-producing bushes could not grow large or fast enough to support their insect, bird, and mammal partners because they were being overgrazed by the elk and deer.

Even the river banks had begun to erode, and the rivers had become straighter and faster. When the wolves were returned, the elk and deer were forced to keep moving as they passed through wolf territory, allowing the plant ecosystems to recover. One unexpected result of these changes was that as plants reestablished, they stabilized the riverbanks, changing their shape into a more sinuous, curvier pattern.

The law of interdependence states that species within an ecosystem are dependent on the presence and health of all the other native species in the local system for their survival. Having evolved alongside each other, species have many connections and associations, and these interdependent relationships are not always apparent or even understood by us.

We need to maintain the ability of all species within the web of life to interact and maintain their obvious and not-so-obvious interdependence on each other in order to maintain that diversity. If too many creatures are corralled into smaller and smaller islands of land, cut off from each other, they cannot stay healthy. Now we must step up and build road bridges and tunnels everywhere (including wildlife access tunnels and gaps in all garden boundaries to expand accessible territory), and we have got to stop taking all their resources away. New, less selfish models of living are required.

The law of finite resources acknowledges that Earth has only so many resources available. These resources are not getting replenished by an interplanetary postal system.

When all the peat from the boglands is gone, it's gone.

When all the topsoil is washed into the sea, it's gone.

When all the coral is dead, it's gone.

When all the species we are causing to go extinct are gone, they are never coming back.

We must grasp the concept that the earth has a limited carrying capacity and there are not endless resources to relentlessly extract and rape. Growth is not infinite; growth is controlled by the laws of nature. The doughnut economics model proposed by University of Oxford economist Kate Raworth, which measures the performance of an economy by how well it meets real human needs without overshooting Earth's ecological limits, is the only viable option I've seen. In her book *Doughnut Economics: Seven Ways to Think Like a 21st-Century Economist,* she sketches out a new system of economics that she visualizes in the shape of a doughnut.

The hole of the doughnut is split like a pie into twelve social foundations: water, food, health, education, income and work, peace and justice, political voice, social equity, gender equality, housing, networks, and energy. The doughnut itself is pictured as the safe and just space for humanity, a regenerative economy. The outer edge of the doughnut is our ecological ceiling, beyond which lie climate change, ocean acidification, chemical pollution, nitrogen and phosphorus loading, freshwater withdrawals, land conversion, biodiversity loss, air pollution, and ozone layer depletion. Shortfalls affect the social foundation, while overshoot breaches the ecological ceiling.

"The twenty-first century task is clear: to create economies that promote human prosperity in a flourishing web of life, so that we can thrive in balance with the Doughnut's safe and just space," Raworth writes.

We are not allowing all of Earth's other life forms to maintain their health and survival within these three laws of ecology. It's important for us to understand that we are completely responsible for the huge crisis in nature. Our ecosystems have already collapsed, quietly and invisibly. They have slipped away unnoticed by people who have lost awareness that we are dependent upon the health of the natural world. Humanity, which makes up just 0.01 percent of all life, has already destroyed 83 percent of wild mammals—and in the short time since 1970, we have wiped out 60 percent of mammal, bird, fish, and reptile populations. That's fairly rapid and shocking, now isn't it?

Seeds of Restoration

Old-growth woodlands and aquatic plant communities are the complex and ancient ecosystems where the true seeds of restoration lie.

We have already lost a third of Earth's clothing, her blanket of trees, mostly since 1900. That's an area twice the size of the United States.

Ireland once had 80 percent of its landmass covered by trees, but today, shamefully, just under 2 percent of the country is clothed in native woodlands, and only a tiny percentage of that miserable fragment harbors the old-growth woods. Mostly the woodlands are relatively newly planted and missing the complex diversity found in our minuscule patches of ancient forests. Those besieged remnants are where the multiple layers of native diversity are hanging on by the skin of their teeth, and when they are lost, so are we. These tiny plots of ancient woodland must be protected, expanded, and connected at all costs.

The Woodland League, the Irish Wildlife Trust, the Native Woodland Trust, and many others in Ireland are striving to protect these ancient arboreal treasures, as are many other good organizations, but without government support or even its vague interest, they are fighting an uphill battle. There are undoubtedly similar hero organizations in your part of the world. Please support them if you can.

If you are lucky enough to have any bits of primeval woods on your land, you are a vital patch in our patchwork quilt. Connect to other ARKs with land corridors if possible to allow them to grow outward, and raise money or crowdfund to protect and expand these places.

Also, remember that our seas, with their coral reefs, seagrass meadows, and kelp forests, are crucial for our survival, as the threads of life are all connected to them too.

The oceans are superheroes in terms of supporting life on Earth, generating at least half of the oxygen produced on our planet, absorbing about a third of carbon dioxide emissions from human activity, and storing most of the excess heat trapped in the earth system from global warming—but only if their ecosystems are intact. Ocean warming and acidification are killing off the world's coral reefs, which occupy only 1 percent of the ocean floor but punch way above their weight as vital habitat for a quarter of the fish in the sea.

I recall, when I was young, diving off piers in the west of Ireland into forests of kelp and seaweed. Swimming through their long fat tendrils, frightening the fish hiding in them, I saw that the sea bed beneath was littered with life, just like a woodland floor. Now when I dive in these same places, I open my eyes underwater to see an empty desert, and it breaks my heart. These underwater worlds are being decimated by mechanical harvesting, by overfishing, and by the particularly destructive bottom-trawling fishing methods. These methods of food production are devastating for all life on Earth in the huge knock-on effects they cause, and they need to stop immediately. Profit or a living planet? Choose.

Marine plastic pollution is a shocking modern phenomenon. Microplastics pour out of our fast-fashion-filled washing machines and into the rivers and oceans, contributing to the large island nations of plastic waste floating around out there. This plastic is, of course, filling the bellies of seabirds and sea creatures, strangling them, poisoning them, killing them. Recycling is a concept that was invented by the fossil fuel industry to allow it to continue producing plastic with an ingenious coating of greenwash, driving the illusion that recycling is good for the planet. It just allows them to continue producing more and more of the stuff. Most plastic that is "recycled" ends up illegally dumped in the seas. Out of sight, out of mind. We are creating hell on earth with our "throw it away" culture. Let me be clear: this is not entirely the fault of the end user; rather, it is mainly the fault of the industries driving the production. At least half of the plastic found contaminating the ocean comes directly from the fishing industry. The whole system needs to change. There is no "away." Planet Earth is one big ball of karma coming swiftly around and back at us. What we do to the earth, we do to ourselves.

INDIGENOUS WILD HUMANS

We need to note that 80 percent of the planet's diversity resides on 22 percent of the landmass, land that is managed by First Nations, Indigenous people who still live in harmony with nature. These people must be protected as the last of the human species who still hold the knowledge vital for our survival. Making up only 5 percent of the human population, they are the natural humans, born into old wisdom and understanding of how to live here, existing in balance with nature. They are the ones who can help us remember that we can't ever own the earth, that we are completely dependent upon her abundance and always directly reflect her overall state of health.

Shockingly, there are still consistent and devastating attacks on these lands and peoples from the mining, farming, and forestry industries, supported by political puppets. They are being murdered for trying to protect the natural world. More than 1,700 Earth defenders have been deliberately killed in the last twenty years. Who is screaming about this? Everyone should be!

The devastation from past and current colonization needs to be acknowledged and repaired because wild humans

are vital to our recovery. Their land rights, resources, and independence must be protected or restored at all costs, because with them lie the most diverse ecosystems, the seeds of restoration for the future earth.

How ARKing Differs from Large-Scale Rewilding

Rewilding on a small scale (ARKing) is a little different from the restoration of vast tracts of land that is kindly being done in many parts of the world. ARKs are generally islands, cut off by boundary walls in housing estates, or isolated patches divided by motorways and roads, or surrounded by non-native forest plantations or chemically soaked farmland, neither of which supports much life other than the chosen, economically important crops. It is, of course, critical to help nature recover on large tracts of land, to protect fully intact working ecosystems, but the domino effect of small ARKs being developed everywhere is also going to make a huge difference. ARKs hold patches of life that will someday be the seeds of restoration for the wider landscape surrounding them.

We have only barely reached a limited knowledge and understanding of the creatures we share this planet with, and scientists reckon we have millions of species still left to discover. We call some of the creatures most obviously responsible for maintaining a balance in nature the keystone species and ecosystem engineers. Apex predators such as wolves and sharks are examples. They drive the health of an ecosystem from the top down in a process we call a trophic cascade.

But top-down trophic cascades are not always the case. Some keystone species are not so obvious and take much study and observation to identify, and thus may still be missing in our understanding and consciousness. One simple example is the starfish. In the 1960s the ecologist Robert T. Paine removed starfish from rocky pools along the Pacific coast and observed the results of his actions. Mussels (commonly what starfish would eat) took over the rocky pools, becoming a monoculture, destroying the diversity of the ecosystem, leaving no room for other life to thrive. The starfish held the balance, and without them, the imbalance caused the system to collapse. So many surprising connections and relationships like this are overlooked without investigation and knowledge.

It's important to understand that because ARKs are usually small, they are missing the keystone species vital for the full range of diversity to exist. We cannot introduce wolves into our ARKs, or other mammals that would not survive in such fragmented habitats. Many species need upwards of 1,500 acres (607 hectares) to have sufficient

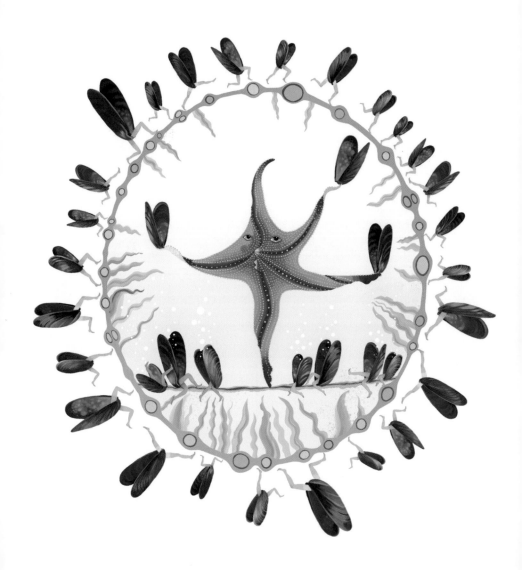

territory to survive. Therefore, we must become the wolf, the deer, the beaver and provide the missing ecosystem services in order to support as many life forms as possible in their absence.

You may know a little about local ecological systems and the roles of various species in your part of the world, but if you don't, you can simply take on the role of a multitasking ecosystem engineer. It's not as complicated as it sounds—it's simply about aiming to create as many stages of ecosystem maturity and habitat as possible in your ARK, because small ARKs are missing the creatures that would create a balanced situation naturally. The ARKing aims discussed in the next section follow from this.

We have removed or decimated populations of the keystone species from most of our land and water bodies because they were a food source, or we saw them as a threat to our well-being or as competition to our food sources. In our ARKs, we must step in and provide whichever surrogate ecological services are required to allow this system to find its full potential, or as close as we can manage without the presence of a full circle of life. Every little bit helps.

ARKing Aims

If you leave land alone, it will slowly heal itself through nature's own succession process. However, this process is dependent on the absence of non-native invasive plants, the presence of healthy soil, the weed-seed bank being viable, and finally the influence and close proximity of a mature native woodland system that can sprinkle its resources your way. These conditions are often missing in these small patches of land we call our ARKs.

On a healthy piece of land that was left to take a breath, the weed-seed bank would emerge as the first line of defence. An ecosystem of pioneer plants would work to restore healthy soil and all its support systems. Soon after, a thicket of thorny plants would shoot up among the heroic weeds to protect fast-growing native trees, which would emerge and further sustain life and promote health, giving way eventually to the large native trees. All stages of an ecosystem are subject to natural disturbances, such as large disruptive mammals or small wildfires, which ensure the whole range of habitats and levels of maturity are always present, creating the maximum abundance of life.

This is nature's intention.

The result is a diverse mixture of native woodland and groves, open meadows, and other layers of rooted and unrooted creatures—full ecosystems that maintain the diversity of life. The earth, like ourselves, is in a constant state of death and renewal. Life in all its forms has adapted to specialize in finding safety and habitat in various stages of this life-cycle system of the earth.

The most diverse places in any ecosystem are the edges, where two different ecosystems meet—for example, where a meadow meets a thorny thicket. The regions where the edges overlap are called ecotones, and these areas support species from both habitats as well as their own unique residents. The ideal outcome is to create as many edges and ecotones as possible, encouraging the widest range of stages of ecosystem maturity and habitats as we can realistically fit into the ARK. If we have the ability and energy, the idea is to encourage as wide a range of habitats as we can manage, to allow for meadows, rocky places, scrubby thickets, diverse native woodlands, wetlands and pond systems, and so forth—as much diversity as possible. This is the way we can support the most creatures.

THE HANDS-OFF
APPROACH TO ARKING

There are many ways to create an ARK. You can just let your ARK go wild to follow its own path, but only if you endeavour to remove the non-native invasive species as a bare minimum effort. We want "lazy" gardeners to use We Are the ARK as an excuse! Whatever your reasons for rewilding your land, we don't mind, as long as you can share it a little. The hands-off approach *can* lead to ecosystems coming back into balance to some degree, but it probably won't support as many creatures or come back into balance as quickly as it could if it had a little more help.

However, if setting it free is all you can manage, it will still be a much better sanctuary than a contrived and controlled garden. A big thicket of unruly brambles is a wonderful ARK, for example; a big tufty overgrown patch of native grasses makes a great home for many small creatures or even ground-nesting birds. We need to do what we can. All efforts are appreciated and gratefully received by our shared kin, striving to survive alongside us two-legged creatures in this beautiful Earth home of ours.

Here are some examples of edges and ecotones that would be full of diversity:

* where woodlands meet open glades
* where mature woodlands meet scrubby young woods
* where scrub meets meadow
* the edges of any water bodies (rivers, seas, lakes)
* where estuaries meet the ocean
* where rocky outcrops meet a forest or meadow

Depending on your available space, aim to create as many of the following habitats as possible:

* mature native woodland
* wildlife pond of any size
* wetland / bog garden (if you have peaty soil already)
* scrubby, thorny thicket of trees and shrubs and tufty grasses and weeds
* areas of disturbed ground to allow space for annual weeds and other magic
* areas of dead wood, log piles

- ✿ ephemeral pond

- ✿ ARK meadow

- ✿ heathland

- ✿ sand and earth banks

- ✿ rocky outcrop, rock pile, or dry stone wall

- ✿ native hedging

- ✿ mown paths through meadows

All of these supports for diversity are described in more detail later in the book. Whatever you can manage in your patch is going to be a huge help in a world of tidy, barren gardens, boundaries, and barriers. Just do whatever you can. I will suggest lots of options and supports in the pages ahead.

ARK Design
and First Steps

It's all a matter of intention, really. When your intention dial is set to "How can I support life to thrive alongside me here?" rather than "How can I impress the neighbours?" or "How can I create an edgy, modern outdoor room?" then you are building an ARK, not a garden. You are part of the solution.

It is possible to turn almost all of your garden or land into an ARK. You can still design pathways, dining areas, nighttime spaces, lawns and patios, and food-growing areas. It just means you approach it all differently, embracing nature as a partner in the process.

If you are developing an ARK on a bare site, the planting will mostly be self-willed if possible. In many parts of the world, though, especially in urban areas, we have done so much damage that we need to step in and guide the direction of the emerging plants. This means we need to remove any non-natives that appear and add as many missing natives as we can, to increase the strength of the sanctuary over time. The more diverse and natural the range of native plants in your ARK, the stronger a sanctuary it is.

First Steps in Building Your ARK

I'm going to break ARKing down into simple steps for you here so you can help rebuild the natural world patch by patch. Your ARK will require its own unique set of supports to restore as much habitat and sanctuary as possible, but these basic general guidelines will start you on your way no matter which part of the world you live in.

Declare your ARK intentions

Put up a sign to make it clear that this patch of land has a purpose and to share what you are doing. Use whatever materials you can find to make yourself a sign stating, "This is an ARK–an Act of Restorative Kindness to the earth." The simple act of erecting a sign changes everything. It enlists you as a proud member of nature's green army–her front line and her rear guard.

A modest homemade sign empowers you as the land's guardian and supports you in allowing it to be a sanctuary. It removes the shame of having a messy garden, which is very difficult for many people to overcome. It explains to your neighbours what you are doing, and you can hope it inspires them to come on board too.

I know in some parts of the world it is not easy to give your land back to nature, especially in places where local government and neighbourhood committees have many rules that make ARKing impossible. But keep the faith, because every organization now has people in it who are waking up to the problems we are facing. It may take only a conversation with one of them to create a wave of change.

Your ARK can still look like a tidy garden but have the basic life support systems in place. Little by little you may find acceptable ways to add wildlife supports such as ponds or log piles, or even just to let the leaves lie beneath your trees and shrubs. Maybe when people start to see your garden full of birds and butterflies and wild plants, they will come over to the ARK side of the fence.

Be creative with your sign! Resourceful people all over the world are getting inspired. Some signs, like my own, are simple declarations on a piece of wood. Others are painted with a selection of the creatures who have arrived at the ARK and made it their home. Listing the species who have returned as an information panel helps people understand the complexities and importance of a "messy" native plant ecosystem. We have seen many beautiful signs made of wood, metal, clay, stone, and recycled tiles and pottery—whatever you can imagine recycling or using.

Add the website address (wearetheark.org) clearly for passers-by or interested neighbours to research the concept and help them understand that there is a good reason for what they may see as a messy garden. Once your sign clearly displays the reason for your wild patch, it instantly gives your ARK purpose and meaning. Now you can be proud, and everyone who sees it can research the We Are the ARK project on the website. You and your land are connected under the umbrella of our caring community.

We love the miniature signs people make for their ARK window boxes. These mini ARKs are often the most heartwarming, providing, as they do, sanctuary, food, and resting places for insects that might otherwise be lost in a sea of concrete. Remember, even if you can give only a small portion of your garden back to nature, it will be a huge help. All donations of land and water bodies returned to wildness are welcome and important, any size, anywhere.

I am looking forward to seeing some more creative productions! Spread the word and share your signs online if you would like to, using the hashtags #thisisanark and #letsbuildanark so I can find them. I will repost as many as I am able on my social media sites.

Ditch the chemicals

There is *no* place for poisonous chemicals in an ARK. They cause many more problems than they solve and are very destructive to life on all levels. Slug pellets kill the birds and small mammals who eat the poisoned slugs and snails. Rat and mouse poisons are leading to a collapse in populations of owls and other large birds of prey, who feed on their poisoned bodies. There is *always* a residual effect from the chemical "solutions."

While this may be a challenge, don't buy plants from sources that grow them using chemicals or peat. Fungicides, pesticides, and herbicides will undo any good work you are hoping to do. Pollinators get ill collecting pollen from plants and soil treated with sys-

temic, persistent chemicals from seed to sale. Ask your garden centre or nursery whether the plants were grown organically and peat free. If not, move on, but before you go, encourage them to set up an ARK section in their garden centre—a transition concept.

As your ARK ecosystem comes back into a balance, the use of chemicals will prove to be unnecessary. Natural predators will return alongside the growing native plant diversity and keep populations of any "invaders" in line.

Break down the barriers

Wildlife cannot move easily through fences or walled-in gardens. The creatures are cut off from sources of food, sanctuary, and suitable mates. The collapse of wildlife populations can be attributed to the islandization of wild habitats. Small wild mammals such as hedgehogs have territories that can stretch from 10 to 50 acres (4 to 20 hectares), and if they cannot move between our isolated ARKs, they are hugely stressed.

If you have boundary walls or fences, perhaps you could discuss it with your neighbours and if they agree, get a contractor to drill a hole or two in the base of each

WE ARE THE ARK

boundary (checking that you don't destabilize them structurally) to allow the free movement of creatures between gardens. Often all you need is a hole the size of a CD case.

You could also excavate a tunnel under your fence in a suitable spot. If your neighbours are on board, gradually replace solid boundaries with wildlife corridors of native hedgerows, which also provide safe nesting habitat.

Reduce hardscape

Reduce the amount of hard landscaping to a bare minimum, to let the earth breathe as much as possible and to create the maximum amount of space for life to be supported.

For the hardscape you do need, try to source reclaimed stone or brick, or perhaps get creative with recycled materials. More extraction from one part of the world to fulfill your needs in your part is not helpful and is usually pretty catastrophic at source. Just do what you can manage, and try not to load guilt on yourself. Use path and patio surfaces that allow the earth to breathe if you can. Bare earth paths are feasible in some warmer climates; mown or bark mulch paths work well for me, and making your own mulch from a coppiced, fast-growing woodland area (if you have the space) is very useful and simple.

70

Slow down the water

Nature abhors straight lines. If you have a river or stream on your land that has been straightened out, it may have seemed like a good idea at the time, but now we know it's an ecological disaster. Removing the bends makes a natural river into a canal. Water moves through it much more quickly, increasing erosion and heightening downstream flood risk. It becomes hard for gravel bars and riffles—which slow the flow and help draw oxygen down into the water—to form. Washing away the smaller gravels also has a hugely negative impact on wildlife, as these gravels are home to many invertebrates and are where salmon and trout spawn.

Restoring the stream or river back to its original wiggly course helps reboot the ecosystem, restores habitat for trout and salmon, and much more. This is an undertaking that requires a good understanding of the ecology of your specific river, but it's worth the research effort. Going back to the abundant edges idea, the wrigglier the watercourse, the more edges and ecotones are available. Restoring native tree cover along waterways also cools down the water and stabilizes the banks.

Remove non-native invasive species

About 250 years ago, people with means developed a taste for plant collection and travelled around the world on great adventures seeking them out. They arrived back with exotic species that they planted to populate their estate grounds and botanical gardens. Native plants were considered common and associated with poverty. Many of these imported plants became the common garden species you may know and love in your part of the world, but many became invasive and what we call garden escapees.

Nobody realized at the time the potential consequences of moving plants or creatures out of their own locally evolved food web, where they were adapted to be part of a balanced system. Many non-native species had no limiting factors in their adopted lands and became so successful at reproducing that they unwittingly became ecosystem destroyers. Most spread by seed or plant fragments, and once they are established they can often outcompete the native flora and fauna.

In the United States, cogongrass (*Imperata cylindrica*) is considered the worst invasive species of them all. It causes ecological, economic, agricultural, and forestry systems to fail when it gets a foothold. Even with this knowledge, it is still being sold in garden centres across the states. The horticultural industry is seriously disconnected from the effect on the natural world of gardening with non-natives.

One of many Irish examples of problems caused by non-native invasive plants is *Rhododendron ponticum*. Introduced to these islands sometime in the eighteenth century, it does very well in acidic soil in mild and damp conditions, where it easily outcompetes native plants by effectively blocking out their light. This in turn leads to a collapse of local ecosystems as the associated native animals and insects lose their favoured habitat. Only the trees that have developed to maturity before the invasion of the rhododendron, those that can grow higher than the rhododendron, can survive. But these have only a short-term prospect, as there will be no more reproduction, no tree seeds (or other layers of a healthy woodland system) to germinate to lead to future generations. The rhododenron's

SHOULD YOU REMOVE NON-NATIVE GARDEN PLANTS IF NOT INVASIVE?

Dedicated ARKevists will be eyeing their pretty imported plants that are not invasive and wondering if they should be replaced with natives.

Weigh up whether the plants you are considering removing are supporting enough creatures or whether it would be wise to replace them with a variety of native species instead. You can take your time with this. Watch the plants in question and see if they are homes to any creatures. A non-native evergreen shrub, for instance, may provide valuable cover for birds or shelter for small mammals. Perhaps install a motion-sensor, night-vision webcam and observe what activity happens in them after dark too.

Making the decision to remove a plant can be difficult, a bit like being the tough parent, but it will get easier. As your ARK fills up with life, you will get braver. Just remember that all these plants are living beings, too, so be respectful if you are removing or reducing them.

All creatures are precious, but it's our job to support nature now in these times. We have done too much damage, and she needs our help to recover. Sometimes that means tough, oftentimes painful, decisions. Use the dead plant material to build dead hedges and log piles to support other life forms.

big showy flowers also poison the native honeybees that collect pollen from them.

In your ARK, I ask you to take a hard line and remove any non-native invasive plants, as they don't support rebooting the local web of life. This is a difficult undertaking on a large scale, but on our individual patches of earth we can manage it easily enough by hand, as these plants do not move at 100 mph.

You might even consider gradually removing those non-native plants you have in your ARK space that are *not* particularly invasive. The truth is that native plants are what builds any ARK.

Allow native plants to invade

One question I am always asked when I give talks is how to handle an invasion of *native* plants such as docks or buttercups in the first years of a developing ARK. These plants are native to Ireland, but they don't seem to allow room for anything else to grow at the time. My experience is that nature knows what she is doing to heal herself when she is working with her native palette, and we should trust her processes.

On my own land, the first year it was under my care
I had horses spend the summer grazing the land down
to a stubble and generously rebooting the land's fertility
naturally. The year after that, my land produced nothing
much other than buttercups and the non-native agricultural grasses that my father had sown years previously. I
was a bit devastated the following year to discover that I
faced an ocean of docks. Little else was growing other than
docks and the remaining buttercups and grasses. The next
year was still just docks, with less area of buttercups and
grass, but in the years after that, more species began to
slowly emerge, such as willows and alders. More diversity
slowly crept in, with different plants carrying out unique
functions of healing and restoration.

I carefully watched what was missing and added in
some more diversity to help support the emerging ARK.
The grass continues to need removing in spots around the
field to create patches of wild resources, islands of native
trees and shrubs, which can now spread outward from
each patch. I see the brambles, shrubby willows, and gorse
slowly making their way in from the edges, dominating
the grass and allowing more space for diversity. I restored
a pond that my predecessors had filled in, divined some

springs to feed it, sourced some native water plants, and watched while others emerged from the depths of the forgotten ghost pond.

It's a magical work in progress, and I have built a home for myself and my kids in the middle of it. I intend to love and guard it fiercely for as long as I am able.

Reconsider the lawn

The ubiquitous lawn. People love their perfect outdoor carpets, don't they?

Lawns are not mandatory, however, as surprising as that may sound. They are a remnant of a long-gone class system. Only wealthy folk could originally afford to have land where they were not growing their own food. This concept exploded after the Industrial Revolution when the masses quickly began to have lawns as a status symbol, to show the neighbours how well they were doing. How wrong we were to see an intentional disconnection from growing our food as an advancement in human society! To me a garden of mostly lawn is a symbol of disconnection from and suppression of our wild nature. A major step backward. Devolution.

In North America, 40 million acres (16 million hectares) are mostly under lawn enforcement for no other reason than neatness and control. These green deserts are usually monocultures of non-native grasses. What an amazing amount of habitat we could restore if we ARKed even half of those lawns! That would change the ecological footprint of the entire continent, creating corridors and resting places for our beleaguered wild kin.

Lawns should mimic woodland glades. Instead of non-native monocultures of grass, they can be transformed into carpets of short wild native grasses, along with wild native herbs and clovers. The border can be a wild ARK meadow or a native wildflower meadow if the seed bank is missing.

Mind your cats and dogs

We love our pets, our fluffy family members. However, these invasive non-native creatures we love so much can have a catastrophic impact on native wildlife.

Cats are highly efficient predators and are responsible in large part for the extinction of numerous reptiles and birds. Cats kill an estimated billion birds a year in the United States. If you are feeding your pet cat, there is no need to allow it to hunt creatures in your ARK. Keep it as an indoor pet, or if you must let it out, fit it with a safe harness or a colourful collar with an efficient bell attached to warn creatures away from it when it hunts.

Dogs are also ecosystem disrupters. It took me a while to realize my dog was causing stress to other unseen creatures when she was young. Digging under brambles as she did, chasing away hares, or pouncing on shrews and frogs may have been a great game for her, but it was a matter of life and death to them. So it's best to be aware that their levels of access to your ARK will take a heavy toll on the safety and sanctuary of your besieged wild family.

For dogs and cats alike, flea treatments are having a devastating effect on water ecosystems. These highly toxic insecticides are ending up in rivers and streams through two main pathways: when the animals are bathed and when the animals swim in rivers and streams. Researchers in the United Kingdom have found the highest levels of the toxic chemicals fipronil and imidacloprid in the rivers downstream from water treatment plants, which indicates it is pets in urban areas that are causing the problems and not animals on farmland.

WE ARE THE ARK

Please avoid using chemical flea treatments on your domesticated creatures if you possibly can. Try to find less damaging alternatives such as preventive treatments containing peppermint oil or diatomaceous earth.

Landscape ARKitecture for Different Parts of Our Shared Planet

Every ARKevist faces different challenges. Every situation will have different resolutions and each site will be unique. But regardless of the circumstances, agroforestry and permaculture have many of the solutions already. You can apply these well-researched and practiced principles on small patches of earth too. Ecosystem Restoration Camps provide examples of doing incredible work on this all over the world.

Building ARKs in dry lands

You may be building an ARK in a part of the planet where desertification is a major issue, the result of deforestation and overuse of land through destructive farming practices. Relentless chemical farming and ploughing of land, while putting nothing back other than petrochemical fertilizers, has led to the death of our soils. Removal of the native plants and trees protecting the skin of our earth has led to 75 percent of our topsoil being washed or blown away in the last century. In many parts of the world where life can extremely challenging, every tree, shrub, and root for miles will often have been removed to use or sell as firewood to eke out an existence.

If you are trying to build an ARK in a dry part of the world, the solutions are simple. Rains, when they do eventually come along in these arid places, can come suddenly in great flashes and floods. This can be extremely destructive, washing away the soil, defenceless without its protective skin of plants. But if you create ways of slowing the water down, giving it a chance to absorb rather than run away, pioneer seeds and plants can get a foothold and start building soil again. This is your best and first step to building an ARK on dry lands.

This can be done with stone ditches or swales and berms dug out and built along the land's contour lines. These allow the rainwater to gather and pool, giving it a chance to percolate downward, raising the water table and creating resilience. This makes it possible to introduce pioneer species of plants, supported by heavy mulching. Pioneer plants are those that usually appear first on damaged land, typically hardy native species that are already perfectly adapted to the conditions and climate of the region.

On a smaller patch, you can create an oasis of hope in the desert and inspire others around you to do the same. Large-scale projects will work only if they are led by local people and not imposed upon them by outsiders. Giving the locals ownership of the plan of work will ensure that it leads to a better life for them alongside the native wildlife. I urge you to research permaculture expert Geoff Lawton with his Greening the Desert Project in Jordan for inspiration.

Windowsill or balcony ARKs

What if you have only a windowsill or a small balcony? Don't worry, there are still things you can do to support our wild creatures. Your little ARK can be an important motorway stopover station for our beleaguered wild plants and insects, making little safe and supportive island oases in concrete jungles. You can provide space for native weed seeds in your window boxes and pots, and many other supports.

Fill window boxes and pots full of organic peat-free compost or soil mixes. Collect weed seeds locally and grow them in your containers. Here in Ireland, they could be mixtures of thistles, nettles, wild grasses, and such. If you are hoping to support particular moths or larvae, you can research what their specific larval food is and add some into your window box. In the United States, for example, growing milkweeds is a great support to the dwindling monarch butterfly populations, as they have a specialist relationship.

If you have no weeds growing near you to harvest seeds from, you can usually find online some great sources of seeds for wildflowers or wild herbs. Just make sure they are as locally sourced as possible as well as organic and native; otherwise, it's not ARK fare.

Sow the seeds between late spring and early autumn. There's no point in sowing them in the cold, as the soil won't be warm enough to germinate them and they will just become bird food. When they grow and mature, you will be so heartened to see insects landing gratefully to feed and rest at your magical motorway service station.

You can also have a bird feeding station. It is just a wonder to have these fluffy, magical, and unique characters visiting every day, way better than television. Make sure any seed in the bird food is not coated in chemicals, which is often the case. If it is certified as organic bird feed, you should be okay.

A miniature birdbath may also be possible on a balcony, if it is sufficiently secured or hung from above and if you clean it out every week with a scrub and some fresh water. Remember that birds can't bathe in water deeper than their legs. Often in cold weather, unfrozen sources of washing and drinking water are hard for birds to find.

Make a teeny "This is an ARK" sign for your pot or box and stick it up somewhere visible to visitors and neighbours in order to spread the idea.

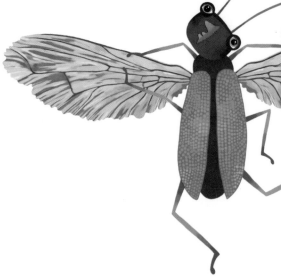

Small urban ARKs

Below is a list of supports to add to a small urban ARK. Many of these supports are discussed in more detail later in the book. Your ARK may be big enough for only a few of the ideas listed. Every small thing is welcome!

❀ Lift any excess or unnecessary existing hard-scape—any paving, tarmac, or concrete—if you are allowed by your local guidelines. All efforts to let the earth breathe and the native weed-seed bank emerge are great.

❀ Add any mixture of small native weeds and plants that you can fit in your plot. You may be able to fit only one or two levels of plant habitat in there, but all endeavours are appreciated and gratefully received by our shared kin.

❀ In tiny yards, often the sides of houses and surrounding walls or fences are the main canvas for ARKing. Native climbers, dead hedges, bird and bat boxes, and rock piles can all use walls as their support structure.

✹ Open connection tunnels for small mammals in boundary fences or walls, with permission and capable help. If all your boundary neighbours agree to the project, you can go a step further and gradually replace solid boundaries with a living, mixed, native hedgerow. This is always a wonderful habitat and pantry.

✹ Sink a small bowl of water into the ground, with homemade ramps to allow creatures to escape if the sides are steep. Add in some native water plants as a wonderful support that also keeps the water clean.

✹ Grow your food and herbs without chemicals, and support local organic growers, box schemes, and farmers.

✹ Support our feathered friends with bathing facilities and feeding stations to get them through tough times.

✹ Make a bug hotel that is deep enough and is a healthy, clean structure.

✹ Provide earth and sand banks for solitary bee habitats.

- Make a pile of stones or dead wood for habitat creation.
- Remove as many artificial lights as possible from the situation and lobby your local government to retrofit urban lighting with red (or second best, amber) filters, which are much less damaging to the movement of wildlife of all sizes.

A layered habitat for larger ARKs

If you have a bit of space to work with, aim to create a layered habitat with as much diversity as possible (more on this in the next chapter). Begin with an ARK meadow and a shortcut path leading into an area of scrubby, thorny shrubs and fast-growing pioneer trees, and from there leading into a more mature woodland. In between, it would be ideal to have a year-round pond, an ephemeral pond/wetland/bog garden, a disturbed area of ground, and a dry stone wall or rock pile.

Whether you order the layers with the tallest trees farthest away from or closest to the house will depend on your aspect (are you facing north, south, east, or west?) and the part of the world you are rooted in (which will determine the levels of light or shade you require). You may aim to put the taller woodland trees farthest away from you if you are concerned that they might block the light entering the house (unless you are living somewhere where you need trees to shade your house). Layer everything in between and overlap areas with as many wiggly edges as possible. The overlapping edges are where the magic happens.

There are lots of other ideas ahead for the larger ARKs out there, and you can adapt many of them for small-space ARKs.

SANCTUARY

The Plants
That Build
an ARK

We know very little from a scientific point of view about connectivity and communication among our plant kin, but our hearts can feel who they truly are, if we take the time to listen. Plants have families, communities, feelings, and awareness. They communicate through their root relationships with bacteria and fungi, and by passing phytochemicals through the air aboveground. They take care of their young, feed their old worn-out elders, and warn each other when danger is imminent. They have intricate relationships and agreements with the microorganisms, invertebrates, and vertebrates that evolved alongside them.

Plants give us oxygen to breathe, filter our water, clean our air, and feed us. Yet we barely give them any heed unless they look pretty or taste good. At last science is catching up with what our native ancestors understood, that plants are living sentient beings, just like us. We humans are so similar to plants, carrying the same microbiome in our guts as is in the soil, and like plants we have beneficial bacteria covering our skin.

When one thinks of the creatures we have driven to extinction, rarely do we include plants in that awareness. Currently it is estimated that nearly 40 percent of all plants on earth are threatened with extinction. Many plants have lost their large unrooted partners, the big animals required to spread their seed. Some plants are known as the living dead as there is only one sex remaining, so they cannot reproduce.

This is why building an ARK is not the same as building a garden. Your aim is to work with nature as a co-creator, to clothe your land in the plants that have evolved within the local food web. By cultivating native plants to provide as many habitats and levels of ecosystem maturity as possible in your ARK, no matter what size it is, you will be making the best possible haven for wildlife.

Why Native Plants?

Ask not whether a plant is pretty. Instead question how many creatures it will support in your ARK.

Native plants—those that grow naturally in the area where they evolved—are the hands-down winners here. Diverse, interconnected layers of plants specific to every region of the world are the earth's protective clothing of her own choice, the basis of all life above and below her skin, so we need to give them sanctuary in our ARKs. Everything depends on the continued presence of these indigenous plant communities.

Wherever you are in the world, your native plants will provide for the intricate dietary requirements of the other members of the local ecosystem. Sadly, our gardens and landscape supply stores are filled with non-native plants. These plants sever the food web. Many have become invasive species, disrupting local ecosystems and causing havoc in wild habitats.

In our ARKs, we need the native plants to thrive so they can support as much life as possible and sustain a healthy ecosystem. Native "weed" plants, grasses, lichens, mosses, shrubs, and trees are all required to ensure a working, balanced ARK. The foundation stones are the annual and perennial weeds.

NATIVE BERRIES AND BIRDS

Many birds really depend on consuming as many berries as they can to put on weight before the hard winter takes its toll on them. Berries from non-native plants in my part of the world contain lots of sugar but very little fat, while native berries contain up to 50 percent fat. Ireland's songbirds in particular need a high-fat diet to survive the winters. Other parts of the world have native plants with berries that are high in sugars instead of fats, to suit the dietary requirements of the creatures native to the area.

We need to welcome native berry plants into our ARKs to have healthy, supported birds. For us in Ireland that means native shrubs and climbers like native ivy, hawthorn, yew, blackthorn, and rowan. In the United States, Oregon grape (*Mahonia aquifolium*) is important for birds in some parts of the Northwest, while desert mahonia (*Mahonia fremontii*) is integral to the food web in the arid southwestern states.

Luckily there are some fabulous websites and books to help you understand what plants are native to your local area, no matter where you are in the world. In the US, you might start with PlantNative (plantnative.org). For other websites and books, see "References and Resources" in the back of this book.

Wild native weeds

I love weeds. The term is derogatory, but I aim to rebrand it to have the positive meaning it should have. The wild things, the indigenous plants have a fierceness and intelligence that I love. A warrior energy.

Native weeds are the wild rooted beings planted and grown by nature herself—and she knows what she's doing. Weeds are the foundation of an ecosystem reboot, starting the process of healing what's below and above them. They provide many important services and are known as pioneer plants.

Nature scabs over any cuts in her skin with her weed-based first aid plaster. Every square foot of healthy soil contains approximately five thousand weed seeds, needing only a fraction of a second of light exposure to become activated. Leave them to do their important work as they emerge. They provide vital food for insects and pollinators. They shove their feet deep into the soil and draw minerals from deep down, up into their leaves. Once they die back, they remineralize the soil as they rot down into the earth.

As gardeners, we have been trained to pull out the weeds and import lots of pretty plants that have nothing to do with the delicate balance of life in a native ecosystem. Let's celebrate and honour the native weeds in our ARKs, as it's such an important job they do! They are healing the soil and rebooting the ecosystem. We should encourage and admire them, as they are the front line in nature's army. Instead, sadly, we have been trained to nuke them at the first sign of emergence, seeing them as messy, unwanted, and useless. We have been looking at it all wrong.

Specialist insects and their native plant partners

Most insects and larvae have not adapted to the fast changes we have inflicted upon them with our modern landscape plant palette.

Plants have brilliant defence mechanisms that deter insects from eating them. Insects have focused over millennia on becoming immune to the chemicals in the plants they evolved alongside, and 90 percent of insects still eat only these plants. They cannot survive on plants imported from foreign shores that they haven't adapted to at all.

Adult insects can be generalists or specialists. Generalist species can survive and thrive in a wide variety of environmental conditions and eat a wide variety of foods, but it's the specialists that need our help. These are the ones that have a very limited diet and can survive only in a narrow range of environmental conditions.

Specialists are very plant specific—their larvae have evolved and adapted to eat the leaves of perhaps only one or two native plant species. Others can eat quite a few species, a variety of grasses, "weeds," shrubs, and tree leaves, but all have one thing in common—the larvae are overwhelmingly dependent on the presence of their native plant partners. Furthermore, specialist insects have often made genetic adaptations to the area in which you live. (Their tongues might be shorter or longer than those of individuals from the same species in a different region, for instance.) This is why trying to source local seeds and plants is important.

Insect populations have dropped by around 75 percent worldwide. The loss of host plants and native habitats is a

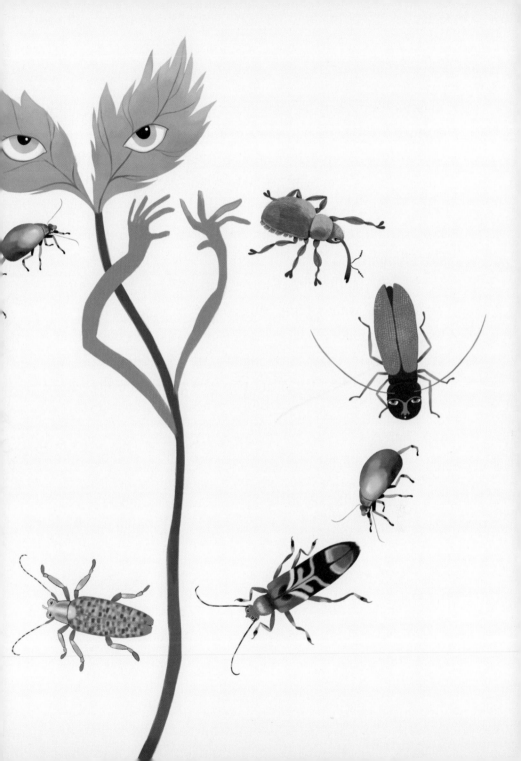

massive factor in this decline, driven by invasive plants and human encroachment on more and more land. Other factors include chemical usage in gardening and agriculture, temperature rise from climate collapse, and escalating layers of pollution. Hence the serious reduction in populations of birds, amphibians, small mammals, and the like who depend on insects for food.

Search locally for books or websites that guide you to understand what plants are needed in your part of the world to support the larval stages of moths and butterflies, otherwise known as baby bird food. See "References and Resources" in the back of this book for some starting points.

CONNECTING THE DOTS
WITH DOUGLAS TALLAMY

Every ARKevist in the United States must get a copy of Douglas Tallamy's books *Bringing Nature Home* and *Nature's Best Hope*. These are essential reading, and you will learn so much! They brilliantly and simply connect the dots among native plants, insect populations, bird populations, the human population, and ecosystem well-being.

Tallamy, a respected entomologist, had an epiphany when working on his 10-acre property in Pennsylvania. He noticed that the native plants were being eaten alive while the non-native plants were untouched. He began the research that led him to conclude that native insects eat only the local native plants alongside which they have evolved. Without the native plants, there are fewer insects, which leads to less food for birds and other animals, collapsing the food web. The solution: filling our ARKs with native plants.

Baby bird food

What is not understood in traditional wildlife gardening is that providing sources of food for adult birds and pollinators is not enough. You must also take into account their reproductive cycles if you want to have a new generation of these creatures. Birds can live on seeds and berries, but that's not what they feed their young. According to Doug Tallamy, 90 percent of bird species feed their young a diet that consists of approximately 20 percent insects and 80 percent larvae. Larvae are also a main food source of many amphibians and mammals, including foxes and hedgehogs.

Birds need to collect three hundred to a thousand larvae a day to feed a clutch of chicks, depending on the species. That's every day, for up to six weeks. Some birds have two clutches a year—how exhausted they must be! This care continues even after the young birds have fledged. Like teenagers, they look ready and independent, but their mums and dads are still feeding them and providing all they need while they practice being grown-ups out and about. That's a serious undertaking.

Both parents start collecting food at dawn and keep going until dark. We observed this from our nest camera at Claire and Joe's Irish Forest Garden in the spring. We couldn't believe the quantity of food the birds were managing to find and feed their offspring! It's only because they cleverly nested in the middle of an ARK that host plants for larvae (baby bird food) were present in abundance.

Without their native host plants, insect larvae will not be present, and the birds will not be able to obtain enough food to successfully raise a new generation. The butterfly survival rate in the wild is only 1 percent, so it's miraculous that they get to make babies at all! They need all the help they can get, I reckon.

If you want to have the magical world of birds in your ARK, you need to support the presence of native plants. Birds carefully choose their nesting sites and many species only harvest food very close to their nests to enable them to keep an eye on their young, so unless you provide the larval food plants, they won't choose your land as a sanctuary. We must support them to feed their offspring so that there will be a new generation, and they cannot do this without an abundance of caterpillars and spiders and such.

A few examples of insect-plant partnerships

Here in Ireland, larvae of the orange-tip butterfly and the green-veined white butterfly have evolved to eat lady's smock (*Cardamine pratensis*) and garlic mustard (*Alliaria petiolata*). Common blue butterflies work with birdsfoot trefoil (*Lotus corniculatus*) to grow their larvae. Holly blue larvae eat holly (*Ilex aquifolium*) and ivy (*Hedera hibernica*) plants, and brimstone larvae need either alder buckthorn (*Frangula alnus*) or purging buckthorn (*Rhamnus cathartica*), difficult enough plants to find in the wild these days. Meadow browns and skippers need wild native grasses.

Stinging nettles (*Urtica dioica*) are among my favourite additions to any ARK. They have specialist relationships with the larvae of the red admiral, the peacock, the small tortoiseshell, and the comma butterflies, and many more. Without nettles, none of those beautiful creatures would exist. Nettles are also my favourite choice of vitamin and mineral tonic for my family, an easy source of many important nutrients missing from our food.

Ragwort supports more than thirty species of invertebrates. One example is the beautiful cinnabar moth, a moth with bright red markings and tiger-striped larvae that would disappear without ragwort. Oak trees are once again the top of the food chain here, as they are in many places in the world, with more than three hundred and fifty specialist relationships dependent upon these trees. In the United States, the milkweed is the exclusive food plant of the monarch butterfly. No milkweeds, no monarchs.

The Plant Layers of an ARK

Because we are missing so many threads of life in our little patches of earth, we are obliged to step in and provide the missing ecosystem services that would naturally create the various stages of ecosystem maturity. We can't really have elephants, beavers, or wolves in suburbia, so we have to mimic their effects to provide for the other creatures dependent on their activities. I call these efforts building the layers in our ARKs. There are the plant layers described here, and other creature support layers detailed in later chapters.

Living soil, fungi, and plants really are nature's foundation stones. These are the basic ARK plant layers:

* short native ARK lawn or meadow
* tall ARK meadow
* scrub and shrubs
* woodlands

Depending on where you are in the world, you may have other more specific layers on your land. For instance, you may have wetlands, bogs, sand dunes, or rocky outcrops, all of which will have their own particular residents. Habitats of all kinds are vital for our varied magical kin to exist.

Regardless of the size of your ARK, the goal is to have as many different layers of ecosystem maturity as possible on your land. You may have only enough space to create one or two layers. Keeping one area as a short ARK lawn and another as a wildflower ARK meadow will still benefit many, many species. Letting some of it become scrub and some become woodland—multiple layers of maturity—is what you should aim for if you have a larger ARK and want to support as much life as possible. All contributions, levels, and versions are welcomed by our fellow creatures in need.

The short ARK lawn or meadow layer

Grasslands are among the world's most important ecosystems, but they have mostly been lost in the last century due to changing farming practices. Many creatures have adapted to depend on this type of grassy habitat. Having a mown path through a meadow, an area of longer grass with a high diversity of native herbs and flowers, will create two very supportive habitats along with their overlapping ecotones.

Short grass mimics areas where wild grazers like ponies would have been present, creating habitats and foraging chances for many species like our beloved blackbirds. It also gives flowers such as daisies and the smaller clovers a chance to shine. Long grass provides safe cover for many small mammals such as mice as well as amphibians such as frogs. Many larvae need to overwinter on native grasses, so best leave them be until spring.

Try to keep mown areas to a minimum, though it's probably best practice to keep a mown or clear area around your house to discourage your ARK family members from moving in. As much as we love them, we don't necessarily want to share our houses with them. Also, if you live in an area of wildfire worries, you will most likely be aiming for a large band of short native plants and grasses in the area around the house.

The rule of thumb for lawn areas is only mow where you go. The simple act of keeping a mown path through the layers of your ARK will allow you access so you can take pleasure in maintaining your relationship with your land. Moving through a natural environment and visiting with it

FIREBREAKS

In hotter parts of the world, you may need to consider fire-breaks and other strategies in your ARK in case wildfires erupt. In a healthy ecosystem, wildfires are part of nature's plan. They create habitats for many creatures, enrich the soil with nutrients, and stimulate certain seeds into life. Some ecosystems are dependent on fire as part of their cycle of life, but the levels of wildfires we are currently experiencing are way beyond the normal range due to the dangerous changes in our climate. In the last twenty years, wildfires have destroyed six times more acres every year than they did throughout the previous fifty years. This is only going to get worse as our climate continues to collapse.

Over millennia, Indigenous peoples in hotter parts of the planet developed a symbiotic relationship with the land and with fire, developing traditional practices to deal with the latter. They used fire management techniques to encourage the growth of plants to increase their crops of food, medicine, fuel, and fibre. This so-called cultural burning is a specialized skill that will be more and more needed in our collapsing climate.

If you live in an area vulnerable to wildfires, do local research on measures to take on your land, referring to Indigenous knowledge when possible. Preventive measures include clearing wide bands of defensible space around your home, placing ponds strategically, using fire-resistant native plants and grasses, and creating dead zones of gravel around your buildings.

WE ARE THE ARK

is vital for your health on all levels. It also creates more edges between layers, increasing the number of ecotones.

A large lawn may be required for practical uses. If you have kids who want to play sports, for example, you may want to keep a patch for them to play on, at least until they grow out of it. These patches of short lawn need not be a monoculture of grass, however. A diverse mixture of native grasses and herbs is a tougher combination and beneficial to boot. It's also much more interesting and beautiful than a bowling green or uniform carpet of lawn. It feels much freer, happier, and more alive.

The tall ARK meadow layer

The next layer of plant ecosystem maturity is a taller ARK meadow.

Different species are supported by various structures of grassland. Tall native grasses, herbs, and wildflowers are an amazing habitat and source of nourishment for many creatures.

These days we are presented with the gardener's version of a flowering meadow, which has a short life span and is a bit of an attack on the senses for me, to be honest.

A taller grassy ARK meadow is a different concept. Again, the intention with this layer of plant ecosystem development is to provide creature support, not to create the traditional gardener's concept of beauty—although an ARK meadow is very beautiful to my eyes these days. A patch of land that is buzzing with life force and excitement is truly beautiful. True nature.

Year on year, native meadows work toward becoming a stable woodland system. Such a system would naturally be disrupted by large herbivores and grazers, who would be checked and balanced by the predators at the top of the chain. In our small spaces, we must carry out the roles of these creatures and try to create as many layers of diversity as possible. Remember, the greater the plant diversity, the greater the diversity of everything else. Keeping an area as a meadow and not allowing it to progress to scrub and woodland preserves this layer of habitat on your land.

The shrubs and scrub layer

Scrub and shrubs form the middle stage in a developing ecosystem. This layer is made up of clumpy grasses, fast-growing nitrogen fixers, thorny shrubby plants, and stands of young pioneer trees. Let those brambles and other thorny natives emerge and thrive. Thorny plants provide shelter from the wind and protection from grazers such as deer to allow saplings to establish. They are powerful deep rooters that remineralize and restructure the soil, and they are also great habitats and food sources for wildlife.

Thorny thickets here in Ireland are made up of beings like bramble, gorse, blackthorn, hawthorn, wild rose, scrubby willows, spindle, and honeysuckles. You will have a different range of native scrub species if you live elsewhere in the world.

Brambles may need cutting back a bit occasionally, as they would normally be kept in check by deer nibbling the young shoots. Most of us don't have deer in our small ARKs. If you don't cut brambles back a bit by "becoming the deer," they can be a little overwhelming and really reduce the diversity in your ARK. Make sure you leave some patches untouched, though, as they are brilliant habitats for many birds and mammals. The ARK sign that directs passers-by to the website will be the key to educating them about how valuable and beneficial these "messy" places are to families of all shapes and sizes.

The woodland layer

Woodlands and forests are the most important habitat, providing homes and sustenance for thousands of species including our most beloved animals. They are home to more than three-quarters of all life on land. Woodlands take many forms, depending on the local soil, latitude, rainfall, and prevailing temperatures. A natural woodland is more than just a stand of trees and plants; it is a living organism, a thriving community of the rooted and unrooted, all completely interconnected, with as big a presence below the ground as above it. Trees are our standing elders, my favourite people.

OAKS AS ARKS

Oaks are truly the king of the woods, and each oak is a valuable ARK. In Ireland, it is said an oak has three cycles: it spends three hundred years growing, three hundred years living, and three hundred years dying as it slowly decays back into the earth and starts again. All stages of an oak's existence are incredibly valuable in the web of life. A truly magnificent soul, an oak protects and nurtures more creatures in its beautiful branches than any other plant does. Native oaks here in Ireland are said to support at least five hundred other life forms when living, and thousands when in the cycle of decay.

Every native tree is an ARK supporting a myriad of creatures above and below the earth. Trees also carry out a water-filtering service that I believe most people do not understand.

Every chemical the pharmaceutical industry creates eventually ends up in our drinking water. There are many routes for these chemicals to find their way into our water, but they always get there. It may be the result of our spitting toothpaste down the sink, peeing out hormones from contraceptives, or washing non-natural clothing containing microplastics in our washing machines. Even the most modern water treatment facilities can't always remove 100 percent of toxic chemicals such as PCBs, fluoride compounds, and sex hormones, so these continue to build up in the water. It can't be good for any human or any other species to drink small levels of chemicals and medications every day.

The members of our tree family are experts at removing these chemicals from water. They have the ability to pull water in through their leaves and up through their roots and to release it as oxygen and water vapour, in a process called the water cycle. A mature oak drinks more than 50 gallons (190 litres) of water a day! The magic happens in between the pulling in and the releasing. Trees process and filter out all those nasty chemicals, including the sex hormones.

Then the magical microorganisms and bacteria that work in partnership with the trees break the harmful chemicals down into their constituent elements. These can once again be released and recycled, causing no more harm. This environmentally sound system for pollution prevention and control is known as phytoremediation.

We need to protect every single tree we already have and plant or preferably allow and support nature to grow *trillions* more native trees if we are to survive the chemical warfare we have inflicted upon the earth, upon ourselves.

Developing a Diverse ARK Ecosystem

Although ecosystems vary all over the world, you can usually build an ARK anywhere using the same basic principles and a little local knowledge and understanding of your climate, native ecosystem, and creature support requirements. Your land may already have everything it needs, but it may also need some help and extra diversity. You might add some plants to your ARK and let nature add others.

The first thing to do when you are building your ARK is to observe your land to see what support it needs. Take your time. Just watch for a few seasons, preferably a year, and see what emerges. Let the land rest until you understand each other. This is ARK time, a slower pace of life.

If your patch of earth is not damaged land, it is most likely already primed with the native seeds the site needs to heal itself. These babies need only a fraction of a second's worth of light to activate. Often all that is required is removing any lawn or paving, or that awful "weedproof" plastic membrane (which leaches plastics into the soil), followed by a light raking to set the seeds free to explode into life.

After that, make sure what has emerged is native to your part of the world. If not, remove it and increase the diversity with locally sourced plants and seeds from native species. To support strong native plant evolution, share native plants grown from seed with your local ARKevist friends.

Then develop as many layers of ecosystem maturity as you can—to make as many homes as possible—and maintain your ARK to sustain these layers over time. It does take a bit of effort to keep most land from reverting to the stable woodland system it's always aiming toward, but remember that your role is to become the ecosystem engineer in the absence of large herbivores.

Sowing or Restoring an ARK Lawn or Meadow

You may not need to sow anything to make a short ARK lawn or a tall ARK meadow. If you already have an old lawn, it may be full of plant diversity, with lots of leafy wild plants scattered through, and you may only need to let it grow long without disturbing it to make a taller meadow. You might be surprised at the range of rooted creatures that are there already if you go out and observe. If you're not sure, you could experiment by leaving the lawn alone to see if it creates

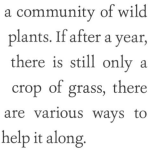

a community of wild plants. If after a year, there is still only a crop of grass, there are various ways to help it along.

The thick mono-culture of grass that gardening fashions have encouraged will have almost no diver-sity and may need support to encourage an assortment of life to creep in. Native wild plants can find it hard to establish themselves in competition with the non-native grasses used in modern lawns. If that is the case in your ARK, you may need to remove the grass and reseed the area with a native seed mix that contains short species of grasses and wild herbs.

If the lawn is not a thick non-native sward but is lack-ing in diversity, you could lightly till or scratch up the surface of the grass in islands and expose the soil beneath, allowing the seed bank in the soil a chance to germinate.

Once the seeds are exposed to light for even the smallest moment, it is usually enough of a catalyst to spark them into action to grow up and become plants. If you find nothing emerges and the grass just comes back, you will need to take a different tack to create some diverse native competition for the grass.

In Ireland, plants like red bartsia (*Odontites vernus*) and yellow rattle (*Rhinanthus minor*) are semiparasitic on grass roots. They weaken the grasses, allowing more room for other plants to creep in and get established. You can try to get seeds of these plants—or whatever equivalent species you may have in your part of the world—to grow in patches in your existing sward.

Removing the grass

Do not spray the grass to remove it. There is no place for poisonous chemicals in our ARKs. So much other life, visible and invisible, gets hurt from these poisons. There are no grey areas here.

If it is a small area, during the growing season cut it as short as possible and then cover the lawn with two or three layers of flattened cardboard boxes, stripped of all tape, overlapping the edges. Soak the card and poke some holes through it so the soil beneath can breathe (otherwise, it can lead to an imbalance in the soil microbiome). Next, cover the damp card with a couple of inches of local soil. For instance, you could repurpose soil you dug out of a pond or a swale. If that's not available, use some organic peat-free soil mix or compost. Sow the native seeds you have collected or purchased (more on that in the next section) directly into it. The lawn will die off beneath the card and the new seedlings will stick their roots down through it if you look after them and keep the soil moist.

For large areas of lawn of a single species, the most efficient way to kill the grass and get back to bare soil is to cut the lawn short and cover it with secondhand black plastic for a year. Pin it down at the sides and use stones or deadwood to hold it down around the covered area. You can usually source a piece of used plastic from a local farmer or builder. There is too much plastic in the world, and reusing it is better than it going into the landfill. You can reuse it for other areas or pass it on to other local ARKevists afterward.

One cool variation on this method that I learned from a great organic grower in Ireland, Klaus Laitenberger, in his wonderful book *The Self-Sufficient Garden*, turns the lost year of black plastic into a productive time. Cut the lawn short and spread a generous layer of well-rotted cow or horse manure over the grass before covering it with black plastic. Klaus recommends a wheelbarrow load for every 3 to 4 square yards (or metres). He then cuts small T-shaped holes into the plastic every 2 yards (metres) and plants trailing squash or pumpkin in there. These will grow and cover the entire plastic area, giving you a great crop later in the year while clearing away the grass at the same time.

The soil may be too rich for wildflowers afterward because of the manure, but it will be perfect for more ARK-like meadows, filled with creatures such as nettles and thistle that are happy to naturally colonize fertile places. Alternatively, you might continue to grow your own food in this area and leave the ARK to other areas of your land.

You can sheet mulch the lawn with other materials to kill off the grass. Old natural-fibre carpets are one possibility. (Modern carpets can be full of chemicals and microplastics, which you do not want to introduce into your ARK.) Thick layers of newspaper (weighed down with rocks and bark mulch) are another.

Reseeding with a native seed mix

Once you have an area of bare soil, you are ready to reboot the meadow layer of your ARK. The best practice involves collecting a wide selection of local native "weed" seeds from land that has a soil, aspect (exposure), and location similar to your ARK. Locally sourced seed stock is the best option to make sure your ARK meadow accommodates insects that have made genetic adaptations within your local ecosystem.

Unless you know your plants, you might need to walk around and make an inventory of wild plants that live in your area and research if they really are native. Just because plants are growing wild, it doesn't automatically mean they are native! Lots of places in the world are completely overrun by non-native plants. This is particularly a problem in North America and Canada. Also, make sure you don't collect seeds from endangered or protected species, unless you have permission and are dedicated to growing new plants to help move them off the endangered list.

Don't get overwhelmed with this process, as it's supposed to be fun. Just collect a few seeds every now and again when you have time to do it, and store them in a paper bag or envelope in a cool, dry place. When you spot a wild plant in the seed phase, do some research, and if it's native, take a little seed. Find out which larvae it has relationships with, and over time you can watch and see if they turn up once the plant has grown.

But all is not lost if limiting factors make it too difficult for you to collect local native weed seeds. You may live in an urban area devoid of wild places, or you may not have access to information about which plants are native. If that is the case for you, the next best way to do an ecosystem reboot is by using an organic native

wildflower or native herb and grass meadow seed mix as locally sourced as possible. These are usually easily available now with a little research. Just make sure they are from a reputable source. Lots of commercial wildflower meadow mixes are not native or organic.

I cannot state this strongly enough: please don't choose a non-native flowering meadow mix, as it will do more damage than good. These mixes result in a big showy meadow of colourful flowers, certainly not what the native flora and fauna need. They are still being sown for our visual pleasure while making us feel that we are doing something great to support nature, a little example of greenwash in the industry. Native meadows develop and change slowly with nature's successional processes, and the plants have evolved within the local food web.

When you have your ARK meadow seeds or a native wildflower meadow seed mix in hand, sow directly into the soil. Do this in the growing season (usually between late spring and early autumn), when the seeds will germinate successfully. If you try sowing them in the winter, they might just become bird food. Not a bad thing, but our aim is to restore living pantries for them and all the other creatures that need it.

Once you sow the seed, keep the soil moist and pro-tect the seeds from birds with netting if necessary, until they have sprouted and are up and running. The seeds will begin the clean-up of the soil and spark new energy in the system.

Maintaining an ARK meadow or lawn

The best ARK practice is to leave the meadow alone until the spring, to leave the seeds on the plants for the birds over the winter and to leave the dead stems as shelter for insects and small mammals. Then, in spring, cut the meadow back with a scythe if possible, or whatever you can manage in terms of gentle maintenance practices. Leave the grasses in a pile somewhere to allow the creatures to escape and then use the material as mulch around your trees or compost it.

If you are keeping an area of short lawn, be creative with its maintenance so that you are living as sensitively as possible as the guardian of your ARK creatures. One option for large areas is to mimic the real deal and borrow some grazers from a neighbour, just like the first lawn maintenance programmes on those large European estates. Sheep were the lawnmower of choice back then, with steep ditches called ha-ha's keeping the sheep away from the house and a scythe keeping a smaller area short. In wet areas, hooves may make for a pretty uneven playing field, but on the other hand, the hooves also create pockets for new habitats by exposing bare soil. Safely containing the sheep mowers in the appropriate zones will be your challenge here.

Fossil-fuel-driven lawnmowers are a problem in them-selves. They create a crazy level of pollution and scare away wildlife with their noise. Consider investing in a scythe or push mower if you are young and strong or have access to willing helpers.

Strimmers (string trimmer machines) regularly cause terrible injuries to our beautiful little mammals such as hedgehogs and many other creatures, too, like frogs hiding in the long grass. Always check the long grass before trim-ming. The time of the morning dew or just after it rains is when frogs are most likely to be hanging around in tall grass. Hedgehogs might be out during the day looking for food just before or after hibernation time.

If you do mow, begin cut-ting the grass in the middle of your lawn and work outward so that creatures have a chance to escape instead of being corralled in the centre. Also, if you *are* using a power lawnmower, leave the engine running for a minute before you start mowing, to warn creatures to run, and do the first mow at the highest setting. Be aware that most robotic mowers tend to be catastrophic for hedgehogs and other small mammals.

Creating a Woodland System

When a piece of land is being ARKed, if it is not damaged, and if it is not isolated or cut off from a source of native woodlands, native tree seeds will most likely emerge as seedlings from the seed bank once the pioneer plants set the stage for them. The weedy and thorny pioneers heal the soil, replace the nutrients, and reestablish an ecosystem, creating protected environments for trees to grow at the right time. In larger tracts of land with a corridor of connection to a natural source of diversity, birds like jays and some other creatures such as squirrels will sow tree seeds naturally as stored food. Luckily, some of their winter storage locations are forgotten, and hence the seeds get a chance to germinate into new trees.

That's just another wonderful example of the intelligence of the web of life. Nature already has every aspect of restoration worked out. However, if your ARK is cut off from local native ecosystems, you may need to plant some pockets of locally sourced native trees and shrubs

to help diversify the habitat. Also, consider planting some heritage fruit and nut trees if you can source local organic stock. These are a great winter larder to support birds and small mammals.

If you don't have a huge amount of land, a native, mixed-species hedgerow will create shelter, safe corridors, and habitat for the families living on the land. You can include many native tree species in a hedgerow, replacing walls and fences with living boundaries. It's a wonderful way to increase the range of native plants in your ARK, creating nesting habitats and safe corridors for creatures to hide in and travel along.

Plant only very young trees, locally sourced seeds, or sustainably sourced cuttings or seeds from native hedgerows, which can be hundreds of years old, if not more. Cuttings—hardwood cuttings in the winter and softwood cuttings in the summer—are basically clones of the parent plant and will never be as strong or resilient as a plant grown from seed. Still, cuttings are handy for making shelterbelts with fast-growing plants like alder and willow, and useful for making harvesting beds for materials to be used in basket weaving and similar crafts.

If you must buy trees from a local nursery, imagine you are adopting a child. The "child" tree will settle in with more ease and adapt more quickly the younger it is. Nursery-grown "soldier" trees–grown straight, like poles, with no character or resilience–often struggle when they are newly planted, as they are generally raised in protected nursery environments. It's often too much of a shock for the poor creatures when they meet wind, drought, and unfamiliar soil in their new homes.

Best sources of seed

Sourcing tree and shrub seeds responsibly from local old-growth hedgerows and woodlands is a good option if done well. Within a ten-mile radius of your ARK is ideal, or as close to that as possible in your personal situation. Try to take a small amount of seed from as many differ- ent specimens as possible to achieve the maximum genetic diversity, for resilience.

Do not take too much from one place, and aim to be responsible. If just a small amount of seed is left, leave it there and move on. You will need permission from the landowner if it is not your land, of course, and be aware

DO YOUR RESEARCH FOR PURCHASED PLANTS

If you are looking to increase native plant varieties in your patch by buying from a garden centre or nursery, take care that everything is grown locally and without chemicals. Make sure the plants are not imported, as this is a totally unsustainable practice that has resulted in the spread of many plant diseases, for trees especially. If the plants are not labelled as organically grown, they probably are not. A lot of the horticultural chemicals used in growing plants these days are systemic and persist in the life cycles of the purchased plants. They damage the soil life and the pollinators that come to feed on them.

Just do your research with your local garden centre or nursery, and encourage them to add a chemical- and peat-free native plant section—an ARK section—to their offerings if they don't already have one.

you may need formal permission if you are taking seed from a registered conservation area.

There are different ways to recognize old-growth native patches. Old maps are useful, place names can help, and finding old-growth indicator species in the lower layers of the woods is the easiest way. Some of the native indicator species are very slow growing and will usually be found only in old-growth native woods. In Ireland, this includes bluebells, greater celandine, and epiphytic lichens and ferns. (Epiphytes are not parasites. They grow on tree branches, living off the moisture and nutrients in the air, as well as the nutrients from decomposing plant material that falls on the tree branches beside them.) Sometimes a certain bird, insect, or mammal can be an old-growth indicator species too.

Collecting seed from native trees that have clearly not been planted is the second-best option. Self-sown trees in wild, rocky places fit this description.

Best times to collect seed

Once you have identified your source of seed, do your research on your native species and find out when the correct time to collect the seed is. Here in Ireland, for example, collecting haws from hawthorn trees too early might mean the seed is too immature, so it's best to wait until October. Birch seed, on the other hand, needs to be collected in August before the wind blows it away. It's different for every region of the globe.

You need to be on the ball to get a few seeds before they are snapped up by our hungry wild creatures. Don't take too many from one place for this same reason and to give the trees a chance for their new generations to be born. The mother trees look after their own young with great care. They support and feed them through the underground network of mycelium. Try to hold this awareness and be respectful when you are collecting seed; be conscious of the sentience of all living beings, rooted and unrooted. Our interference, though well meant, still needs to be acknowledged in each case.

Inoculating and waking seeds up

Out in nature, seeds have to survive against many difficult obstacles, not the least of which is their position as the meal of choice for many a hungry creature. In order to give your tree seeds the best chance of succeeding, you can carry out a couple of steps to support a positive germination.

First, seeds may need to be extracted from pods, wings, fleshy fruits, and cones. Then you may need to wake them up from a natural state of dormancy in a process called stratification. This involves allowing the seeds to be exposed to periods of cold and warm temperatures and protecting them during this time. Some seeds need longer than others to wake up, but you can combine this process with inoculation as described next.

The best support you can give a sapling is to inoculate it with a full range of microorganisms. This can be done by growing locally collected seeds in a replica of a forest floor. In a human body, our health lies in our gut, where our microbiome resides. We are simply inside-out plants, as plants have access to their microbiome through their roots in the soil. If they get a start in life with a full range of microorganisms, they are going to be much more resilient and healthier than any tree grown in sterile soil from a nursery.

The "Forest in a Box" scheme outlined by the Woodland League in Ireland is, in my opinion, the best way to grow trees from seeds. A square-metre wooden box is half-filled with leaf litter collected locally from a healthy native woodland (being careful not to take too much), aiming to reproduce a woodland floor. The box has higher sides to encourage the seedlings to grow up straight and tall as they reach for the light, the same way they would in nature. A fine wire mesh over the box stops creatures from eating the seeds. This mesh lid is removed when the seedlings have reached the top of the top of the box and no longer need so much protection. No soil is added, and the leaf litter in which the seeds are grown is kept damp in a sheltered spot outside. The box is left open to the elements, facilitating the stratification process that is usually required to activate the seeds. (if one is using seeds needing stratification such as hazel or hawthorn, among others).

The Woodland League claims to harvest up to two hundred trees every second year from their larger boxes, working within the local ecosystem with locally sourced seeds. These trees are strong, healthy, and fast growing, having been inoculated with all the fungi and bacteria that should be available to them on a forest floor.

Planting trees out

If you plant trees from seeds, cuttings, or whips, you must nurture them as you would a child. While they are young, they may need support for a few years to become strong and resilient adults.

After they are planted in their new homes, it may help to mulch them to protect them and the soil and give them the best chance possible. My method for mulching is simple. I surround each tree stem with a circle of cardboard 1 to 2 feet (30 to 60 centimetres) wide. (I use two layers of flattened cardboard boxes and make sure all tape is removed. Poke some holes through the card so the soil beneath can breathe.) I put a thick layer of mulch on top (bark mulch is one good option), keeping a little space around the tree trunk and taking care not to pile the mulch against the trunk. Then I add three rough fieldstones approximately 20 inches (50 centimetres) in diameter. These hold down the mulch, and they absorb the heat of the sun during the day and release it slowly at night. The stones also help the little plant avoid being smothered by grasses and hold it solidly in the soil until its roots grow strong, avoiding the need for tree stakes.

This method creates a nursery microclimate to protect the trees and support them. The worms love the cardboard and start to aerate the soil and reestablish its microbial life. The decomposing cardboard also returns carbon to the soil in the process. This is not always the best method for every part of the world, though, so do your own research for your area.

The important thing to remember is that wood chips or mulches are not a long-term solution. They simply give a start to the trees, removing the competition of grasses and other plants that might otherwise swamp them. Once the saplings are strong and up above the height of the grasses, I would encourage you to add a little diversity around their feet, if nature isn't already doing so. Like us humans, no tree is an island. They thrive when living in supportive communities, surrounded by a network of sustenance and company.

Planting pockets of diverse miniature forests in a large ARK will allow the trees to grow quickly in a supportive environment and let them spread out from these islands on their own. It's quite magical to watch them expand outward at their own pace.

THE MIYAWAKI METHOD

A Japanese botanist named Akira Miyawaki observed that native species of trees in Japan—relics of the primary forest, most of which had been cut down—grew around temples, shrines, and cemeteries, where they had not been disturbed. Based on his knowledge of these species, he developed a method to restore native forests quickly by densely planting seeds of native trees. He used this method to successfully restore forests at more than thirteen hundred sites in Japan and beyond, in shelterbelts, woodlands, and woodlots.

The method advocates planting a wide variety of native species saplings very close together. Around three plants per square yard (metre) is recommended, including species that would form the lower layers of a forest floor. The crowded plantings stimulate competition and the establishment of mycorrhizal relationships underground.

These miniature forests are more than a hundred times more diverse and grow more than ten times faster than forests planted by conventional means, resulting in dense pioneer forests in twenty to thirty years instead of the two hundred years normally needed for natural succession in Japan.

Thinning and coppicing

When the trees in your ARK grow tall, you may need to step in to carefully thin a few branches, or even coppice some trees to make sure more light gets through to the lower layers beneath. This maximizes the food and sanctuary available on that land. Otherwise the trees might eventually become a closed canopy without much living in their shade. This mimics the browsing actions of large herbivores like elephants, elk, or bison (again, depending on the part of the world) or ecosystem engineers like beavers. In their absence, it's our job to carry out their roles, to reweave the missing threads in the web as much as we can.

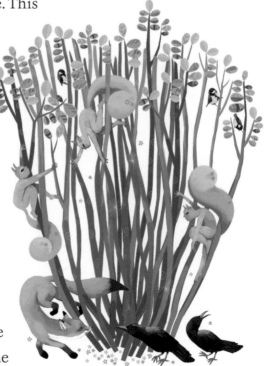

The ancient practice of coppicing is one of the

rare symbiotic relationships that humans developed with nature. This traditional woodland management practice involves felling trees so new stems will grow from the remaining stumps. This practice allowed Indigenous humans to live in abundance in a gentler relationship with the trees and their communities for millennia.

Many trees can be coppiced, and this method is valuable if you have limited room in your ARK. If you cannot manage to fit even one large tree in your ARK, perhaps you can find room to consider a coppiced version of the same tree species. Research whether your local tree species are candidates for coppicing to see if it is an option for you in your part of the world. Most broad-leaved trees can be managed this way, some better than others, but generally conifers cannot be coppiced.

Wait until the tree is well established; you can coppice most trees after five to seven years. Be respectful and let the tree know what your intentions are. Cut the trunk right back to just above where the stem swells coming out of the ground, at about a 15- or 20-degree angle to help the water run off and avoid root rot. This approach creates a more shrublike tree, which can be recoppiced in full or in part whenever it is getting beyond the size you can manage.

Coppicing trees creates access to light so other plants in the lower layers can thrive. Rather than killing the tree, it results in multiple stems shooting up in replacement. These shoots would traditionally be used to make baskets and fences, firewood, charcoal, instruments, and tools.

Extra Layers
of Creature
Support

I feel a terrible grief every time I see how scared the wild creatures are of me, how startled and terrified they are by my human presence in the natural world. Deep in my being, I know there was a time long ago when they were not afraid of us–when we all lived in harmony together and we treated these creatures as sacred. Killing and eating food revolved around gratitude, ceremony, and the promise to live in service to the earth for the lives taken from her every day. Insects were our gods, trees were our gods. Birds, bats, fish, and every living creature that allowed us to live here were all deities to us.

It's time to create safe places for these beleaguered creatures once again. It's time to remember we are simply their servants, their caretakers, completely dependent upon their health and abundance. It's time to build as many homes for them as possible in our ARKs.

Embrace the Mess!

We are losing the magic in the world, in ourselves. We are trained to see wildness in our gardens as messy and lazy, to see neatness as proof of our care. Neatness in nature equals barrenness (or something closely resembling it). A neat garden holds very little diversity of life. There is no magic in a tidy wall-to-wall carpet of lawn and non-native plants. Hope cannot be found in those spaces; sanctuary is not available. The intricate and interdependent relationships that exist among many native plants, fungi, insects, and other creatures are not respected or given room.

Rewilding and ARKing land allows life to thrive once more, even though it might look like a mess to some traditional gardeners' eyes.

Death as an important part of life

The dead and dying elements in nature offer a huge range of support for the living. If you are growing ornamental plants in your garden still, you are usually encouraged to deadhead everything as autumn arrives. But leaving flower and seed heads standing over the winter, unmanaged and uncut, will benefit many creatures in the lean months. The native weed, tree, and shrub seeds along with native berries are especially beneficial to wildlife, helping to sustain them during the cold, dark months.

I like to let wildflower meadows go to seed, and I leave the seed heads and hollow stems standing over the winter to feed the birds and give insects habitat and shelter. Then I cut them back in the spring and gather them up for the composting areas or just leave them in sheltered piles to break down over time.

Similarly, deadwood is critical in supporting a high level of biodiversity. At least 40 percent of woodland creatures

depend on deadwood at some point in their lives. Deadwood has a few different forms: fallen wood (woody twigs and debris), standing and intact deadwood (tree limbs, still attached but dead), and tree stumps. All these types of deadwood have specialized relationships with insect and fungi partners as well as more generalized relationships with a wide range of grateful foragers.

Standing deadwood sustains a huge amount of life. A living mature oak, for example, provides for more than five hundred species of life, but a dead or dying tree supports thousands! If it is not unsafe to leave a dead tree standing, leave it be, with support if required. If you have to take it down for safety reasons, leave it lying in your ARK to decay back into the soil, providing much support to the ARK ecosystem as it does.

Leave the old lower branches of the elderly trees. They often let them droop to the ground to give themselves support when they reach a less stable age. Now, they have to cope with us "tidying up" their lower limbs—removing them in an effort to create clean lines or to open up views. Would you kick a walking stick away from an older person? We should see the elder trees in the same way, because they deserve our reverence and respect.

Log, leaf, and twig homes

If you can get hold of them, throw a pile of logs somewhere quiet and create a log, twig, and leaf pile. Lots of creatures will make homes there. Rotting wood and leaves create warmth for the families that take sanctuary. They need safe places like this where they feel they are hidden from predators and humans alike. In some parts of the world, you will be creating log pile homes for magical creatures like turtles that are part of your ecosystem. I am in awe when I do consultations with people about their ARKs in places like South America, when we discuss things like their alligator problems. What a magnificent problem to have!

Leaves are the earth's winter planet, vital for a healthy ecosystem. Let the leaves in your garden fall where they want. Rotting leaves perform many functions—not least, feeding the plants that produced them. Larvae often need to finish their life cycles in a carpet of leaf litter, falling off their host plants and out of tree lagoons to pupate in the leaves beneath, and many small mammals like hedgehogs burrow in them for winter warmth.

Leaf blower machines are catastrophic to an ecosystem, apart from the obvious noise and environmental pollution they cause. They kill many important teeny creatures with their hot air action, burning alive the larvae and insects living in the leaves. If you need to remove leaves from paths or driveways, a good hard sweeping brush is your best option.

Dead hedges

Dead hedges are stacks of logs, branches, twigs, and old stems that are packed tightly between two rows of staggered wooden posts. They make a brilliant instant windbreak and abundant habitat for many creatures. They're a great way to use coppiced material or hedge clippings. A dead hedge doesn't have to be so rigid in design—it can be a messy stack of dead, woody

material in a pile—but the structure does make a great edging to an area, creating spaces and making sense of your ARK in terms of flow and aesthetic appeal.

Bare earth and sandy banks

Here in Europe, in the past wild boars would have disturbed the soil regularly when they shoved their snouts into the earth, rooting for grubs. Large mammals would also have disturbed the ground with their heavy hooves, especially during boisterous activities such as testosterone-induced fights in rutting season. By doing so, they created niche habitats for many creatures. They sped up the decomposition of organic matter by digging woodland litter into the soil and were important distributors of seeds in their travels. Boars, like deer, are a species that can cause much damage to plant life and diversity when their natural predators are out of the picture. In their balanced state, however, they are hugely beneficial and important players in the maintenance of diversity.

Robins are known as the gardener's friend, always to be seen following any soil disturbance around. This is the robin displaying an ancient relationship it had with the wild boar. It would follow the boar around and find a feast fit for a king in the disturbed ground made by these important ecosystem engineers.

Bare earth provides important habitats for many species and allows annual weeds to get a chance to germinate in these exposed spaces. Insects use it to nest in and bask on, while many birds like a good dust bath to rid themselves of parasites. The more than two hundred species of wild solitary bees in Ireland build nests for their larvae in small tunnels they make in bare earth, sandy banks, or sandy gravel. If you do a little research, you can find out what species of wild bees exist in your part of the world and whether they are threatened and could use your help.

We need to become the boars in our gardens, or whatever your local equivalent is. Occasionally, maybe once a year, use a hoe, a rake, or a trowel to disturb the soil in a few small patches of your ARK, creating hollows and earth banks like a boar would. And build up a raised earth bank and a sunny bank of soft sand and gravel somewhere too. The more habitat diversity, the better.

Rock piles and dry stone walls

Another great habitat support for many creatures is piles of rock, or dry stone walls built without mortar but maybe using a little earth in the centre of the wall occasionally to add diversity and expand the range of habitat. These rocky places become homes to many ferns, lichens, and mosses, important creatures themselves, and many succulents and unusual native plants will happily set root there.

In Ireland, dry stone walls are safe havens for shrews and lizards, field mice, beetles, and spiders. Toads bury under the stones and ground-nesting bees make homes in the crevices. Many mammals take advantage of tunnels inside these piles and often hibernate inside them.

If you have not got the room for a wall, a pile of stones in a sunny spot will go a long way too. You will have fun seeing who comes to live there in your own part of the world.

Water Homes

Water ARKs are so important. Freshwater bodies—rivers, streams, lakes—are often toxic to wildlife, mostly due to agricultural chemical runoff, salt and rubber runoff from roads, tar residue from road work, human sewage and animal slurry being pumped into streams, and general urban pollution. Building a pond, no matter the size, as a source of clean water and habitat is probably one of the most important supports we can offer in our ARKs. Water *is* life, and it is a vital component of any ecosystem support network.

Teeny tiny water ARKs

Even on a balcony or windowsill, a shallow bowl of fresh water is a great support. Add some islands or twig ramps in case insects get trapped in the water with no way out. A tiny pond with a native oxygenating plant or two will be even better. A mini floating solar fountain or bubbler will keep the birds happy and the water moving and oxygenated.

Ephemeral lagoons in stumps and logs

Tiny pockets of rainwater in old hollow tree stumps and decaying wood crevices are habitats for a myriad of microorganisms and insects who like stagnant water and the mossy edges around such places. (Remember that creatures such as lichen and moss need sanctuaries too.) These little pools are called lagoons.

Decay is a rich source of life for lots of creatures. Many larvae, like the drone fly larvae in Ireland, are semiaquatic and live in stagnant pools of water where they consume decaying matter. Many of our important hoverflies, too, need these lagoons as nurseries for their young. In turn, our bats and birds need the hoverflies for sustenance. Everything is connected.

You can always mimic this in your ARK by allowing tree stumps to decay naturally or by making a decent hole in a log here and there and letting nature do the rest when it fills up the holes with rain and rotting leaves. Just make sure you put in an escape ramp or twig for the larvae to use when they are ready to exit. You can also supply a homemade lagoon until your ARK is mature enough to provide the necessary rotting wood and decaying matter in a natural way. Do note, however, that in some parts of the world, allowing places for mosquitos to breed near your home is actively discouraged due to the diseases they can carry.

A HOMEMADE LAGOON TO SUPPORT LARVAE

1. Find an empty plastic jug or an old plant pot without holes in the base or something similar. If you are using a plastic screw-top jug, cut the top off so you have a wide opening.

2. Fill the container with leaves. Make sure you have a stick or a twig as a ramp so the larvae can leave to pupate when they are ready.

3. Make a little hole or two near the top of the container so any overflow can escape without washing out the larvae.

4. Allow the container to fill with rainwater.

5. Place the container securely in a shady spot on the ground and surround the base of it with native tree leaves and old decaying twigs and such. This is where the larvae will pupate when they come out.

6. Keep an eye on the lagoon in case it needs topping up with water in a dry spell.

Wildlife ponds

Wildlife ponds are by far the richest habitats you can provide to support your ARK dwellers. If you have the space and can take the time and energy to install a small wildlife pond, do! It's a huge help to wildlife, second only to native trees. A small pond, even a sunken bowl filled with rainwater, will be a watering hole for the small creatures. Before you know it, newts, water beetles, tadpoles, and dragonflies might find your ARK. (Just make sure it has rocks or twigs placed in it to act as a ramp rising above the waterline, allowing creatures to escape, as they will struggle and may perish with steep, slippery sides.)

Numerous books and websites are dedicated to helping you position and build your own natural pond. Simply put, all you need to do is to decide on your choice of water-retaining options and dig a hole in your garden in the desired shape, remembering that the edges of the pond are the most diverse places. To increase the number of edges and ecotones, design your pond to be very curvy/ wiggly. You can make it as big or as small as necessary to suit you and your ARK.

If you have a huge ARK, an island in a large pond creates a protected space for nesting birds. Allowing a decent amount of open water will give you the joy of watching birds swooping for a drink and bats chasing midges at the surface as the light fades. Make most of the edges around it very shallow so creatures can get in and out safely, or else they could get stuck in there and drown.

To retain water in a pond you must, of course, waterproof it somehow. The options are puddling clay or a good quality pond liner that will withstand the test of time. Bad or cheap liners can be broken down quickly by the sun and temperature changes and will end up in the landfill eventually, which isn't great. Puddling clay such as bentonite can be purchased online, or if you are lucky you might have a clay-heavy piece of land to begin with.

Dig out a pond-sized hole (depending on your ARK and your land) and tamp it down when it has a little water in it, removing any stones that come to the surface. Make it as deep as you can manage in the centre—relative to its size, of course. Deeper water will help keep the pond water cool and balanced. If you decide to use a liner, put a good 4-inch (10-centimetre) layer of sand beneath the liner (to keep stones from piercing it from below) and make sure the edges are tucked well under the surface above the high-water level. You can use stones and pebbles to cover up the exposed liner on the shallow edges, creating even more pockets of habitat.

Puddling clay is a brilliant option, though it can be expensive. The clay comes as a powder. When it's wet, the material swells to more than ten times its original volume. This blocks and seals even the tiny pore spaces in the soil, preventing the water from percolating through. Bentonite should be applied in a layer only about a half inch (2.5 centimetres) deep all over the pond floor and sides, which you can then cover up with a consistent few inches of the excavated subsoil. (Some other clay products need to be covered to different depths.) Tamp this down firmly and fill the pond with water.

If you are working with existing high-clay-content soil like I have on my land, it is a lot easier. The pond simply needs to be excavated and then tamped heavily to seal it. The bucket of the digger being dragged along the floor and sides did the trick in my pond. It suffered a little with cracks around the high water line in the first couple of years as the level went down in the summer, but this was easily solved by my kids, who put on wetsuit shoes and sealed the cracks with a little slippery pressure. It's really messy work, so you'd best embrace it and try to have fun. Get your friends to help. Ply them with food and have a wallow party.

It would be best to fill the pond with harvested rainwater or springwater if possible. The chemicals in modern tap water kill bacteria, and this is not a good thing for nature (or our own microbiome). Bacteria are one of the invisible kingdoms that rule the world and are vital for health in all ecological systems. Maybe you live somewhere temperate like Ireland where the rain will graciously fill your pond up for you, but if not, work with what you have. At the very least, let chemically treated tap water stand for twenty-four hours in a barrel before using it, as this allows the chlorine to evaporate.

Make sure you think it all through. Every situation and climate will present its own issues. You may need to put in an overflow pipe or a channel of gravel to direct any excess water to an area where it can soak away safely, or even into the drainage system. In any case, filter the overflow to make sure it is not washing away any creatures. In the end, it is worth the work. It's just the best entertainment, sitting by a pond and watching all the magical creatures that come gratefully to share sustenance, especially at dusk or at night when the nocturnal worlds wake up to hunt and play.

Installing a solar-powered fountain or bubbler is a good way to let wildlife know the water is there. And it helps oxygenate the water, keeping it fresh and healthy for those who come to quench their thirst, have a wash, or decide to make a home there.

Wetland or bog gardens

A wetland you create or restore will soon be hopping with life. Choirs of birds and amphibians will sing their songs, and visits will regularly be made by dragonflies, bats, and all sorts of magical creatures, depending on where you live in the world.

Ideally, a wetland or bog garden will be situated in the lowest part of your ARK, have shallow edges, and be filled with a rich diversity of indigenous, aquatic wetland plants. If you are lucky enough to have a natural stream, you could become the beaver and build a dam across part of

WATER PLANTS FOR YOUR POND

An adequate number of oxygenating plants can keep your pond from going stagnant. It's important to use only native plants to populate your ARK pond. These plants have also evolved within the local food web and have created many relationships with other native, unrooted creatures. You should aim for maximum diversity of plants—deep-water rooters and edging plants.

Make sure you obtain your native plants from a reputable source. Double-check for obvious animal life hanging around in the pot or any different attached vegetation before introducing the plant to your pond. Water plants easily mingle together, and you do not want to end up with even a scrap of a piggybacking non-native water plant or the eggs of a non-native invasive water creature. These aliens will totally take over and cause an imbalance, the opposite of an ARK.

In Ireland, many invasive creatures have exploded in our water systems, crowding out the native life. Creatures like Zebra mussel (*Dreissena polymorpha*), Himalayan balsam (*Impatiens glandulifera*), and curly-leaved waterweed

(*Lagarosiphon major*) have heavily impacted water ecosystems. These implanted invaders are not part of the food web. I am sure you can easily find out what the problem species are in your local area if you research non-native invasive water plants and creatures.

MOTHER NATURE KNOWS BEST

it to create a small, slightly excavated wetland area, which you could then build up slowly with native wetland plants.

Bird and Bat Supports

Places for birds to bathe and supplementary housing to help birds and bats are important for any ARK. I love seeing wildlife-support homes attached to our own houses. There is something very special about sharing the walls of our homes with these beautiful little souls.

Birdbaths

Birds won't bathe in water deeper than their legs, so a birdbath is a great support to our fluffy friends, especially if you keep it filled with clean water. Birds get to know where the bathing spots are in their neighbourhood, and you will be treated to a fabulous display, the bathing dance. Just remember it's really important to give the bowl a good scrub once a week and keep it topped up with clean water so that the birds don't spread diseases among themselves.

Bird boxes

Birds normally make nests in crevices in trees, but you can also erect bird boxes to offer ready-made homes for these colourful characters and invite them to share your land. You will soon know which locations and types of bird-houses are considered prime real estate. Birds are very picky, no different from us.

A few basic pointers:

❁ Obtain good quality boxes from a decent crafter who doesn't use chemically treated wood or nasty glues. Or make the boxes yourself—there are loads of online tutorials on making bird boxes, and it's a good way to spend some time with your kids if you are looking for an excuse.

❁ Secure them in different positions. Place bird boxes at least 2 yards (metres) off the ground for small birds, sheltered from the prevailing winds and away from strong sunlight, where they will feel safe. A northeast-facing spot is recommended here in Ireland, but as long as they are sufficiently shaded and sheltered, you can try lots of positions.

✤ If you are attaching a box to a tree, make
sure you use strong adjustable ties to
secure it, not nails. Trees hate nails being
driven into them; wouldn't you? Nails do
terrible damage to trees, opening up their
skin to all sorts of infections.

House sparrows like to hang out in communities,
so a few boxes right beside each other will suit them.
I've seen people make a terrace of houses
for these social, feathered creatures.
Cutest thing ever.

Be inventive! You can use old tea-
pots slightly angled downward so they
don't take in water, insulated and firmly
fixed in a way that won't allow them to
shift in the wind and freak out the parents.
The spout may need blocking off from the
inside. Tough old waterproof hiking boots
or welly boots, slightly angled downward so
they don't take in water, also make suitable bird
abodes if fixed firmly in place (without using
nails on living trees, of course).

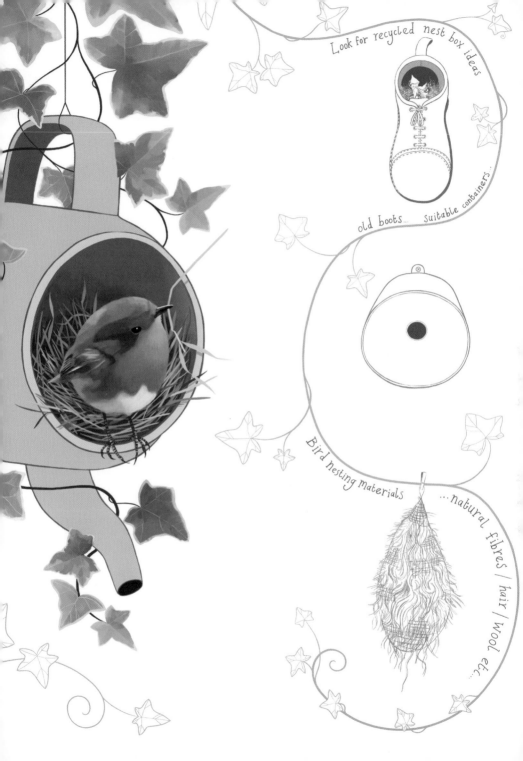

Look for recycled nest box ideas

old boots...   Suitable containers.

Bird nesting materials   ...natural fibres / hair / wool etc...

Owl houses

In Ireland, we have three types of native owls: barn owls, short-eared owls, and long-eared owls. Owl populations have taken a downward dive. The loss of "unimproved" grassland (a farming term for old native meadows) and the consistent removal of native hedgerow habitat has been devastating to them, as it results in a steep decline in their food sources. But the greatest cause of death for owls is consuming mice and rats that have been poisoned by rodenticides.

Long-eared owls like to nest in old corvid nests or abandoned squirrel dreys. Short-eared owls are rare these days. In winter, they can be found in coastal spots or in rough grassland; in summer, in young woodlands.

We were down to 400 breeding pairs of barn owls in the last few years but a wonderful BirdWatch Ireland campaign thankfully led to an increase to between 500 and 650 breeding pairs. Still so few. These beautiful creatures make their nests in old ruins, barns, disused chimneys, the attics of old buildings and churches, tree holes, and rock crevices.

GET A LOOK AT WHO'S COME TO STAY!

Set up a motion-sensitive night-vision camera to catch sight of the families that take shelter in your ARK. If you have a pond, grow a living willow structure beside it to hide inside so that you can watch firsthand the wild parties that happen when humans are in dreamland.

You could also erect a homemade house for them. Sadly, owls regularly get hit by cars and trains, so it's probably best not to encourage them to live with you unless you are far away from a busy road. If you live in the countryside and have a mature tree with a thick trunk, a high canopy, and few or no lower branches, on the edge of a woodland or standing isolated, you have an ideal place for a barn owl house. A tree inside a woodland is unlikely to attract a barn owl.

The house needs to be erected at least 3 yards (metres) above the ground. The access hole should face open ground but should not face into the prevailing wind. The owls won't like it if the access hole is screened by buildings or other branches or leaves. You can always follow a book or online tutorial to build one or just buy one from a good crafter who uses untreated wood and no nasty glues.

Bat boxes

Bats make up a fifth of our mammal species but are quickly losing numbers. This is due to loss of native foraging and living habitat, chemicals in our garden and agricultural landscapes, and urban lighting, which is decimating their nighttime insect food sources. (More on this in the next chapter.)

You can either buy a bat box from your local wildlife trust or garden centre, or build one yourself. Buying one is much easier, as you really need to know what you are doing with bat boxes. Place the box at least 3 yards (metres) off the ground, on a tree or on the eaves of your house, in a shady position. Locate the box away from artificial light and provide an access hole the bats can directly fly into. Bat species are protected in many countries around the world, so it's important to never disturb them once you have erected the box.

Minding the Tiny and Invisible Kingdoms

I feel blessed and honoured by every insect I see in my ARK, excited they have come to visit or stay, because now I understand how vital they are. But gosh, these guys have had a hard time from us humans, being the stuff of nightmares for so many. Just as weeds have gotten a bad reputation in conventional gardening, bugs have been given a bum rap. Moreover, gardens have become food and reproductive deserts for many species of insects, filled with non-native plants we have introduced solely for our visual pleasure. I aim to change your mind on all that.

Reversing Insectageddon

Insects are up against many factors leading to a steady decline in their numbers. These include the horrendous overload of chemicals we have consistently dumped and sprayed onto the earth, the spread of alien invasive species, and the vast deserts of chemically treated tree and crop monocultures that not only don't support insects but also actively weaken and kill them. Of course, overarching all of these factors is a collapsing climate.

All these impacts added together have caused what is aptly named Insectageddon. We are sadly and suddenly 75 percent of the way down the road to human extinction. This is because we have lost 75 percent of the biomass of our insect populations, mostly over the last fifty years (the era of chemical agriculture, forestry, and horticulture).

When they go, we go.

It really is as stark as that.

The decline of insects must be reversed immediately, as they are the basis for the whole food chain and the web of life. The ecologist E. O. Wilson (Half-Earth Project) suggested from his studies that we would last just months on the earth without insects. They pollinate nearly 75 percent of all crops and 90 percent of all flowering plants on this planet. Without them, there would be an unimaginable catastrophe within a short time. The inability of plants to reproduce without their partnership with insects would quickly lead to a barren planet.

Insects are also vital to the health of freshwater and land ecosystems, carrying out fundamental services in the life cycles of fish, frogs, and lizards. They are an important

source of food for many
mammals like hedge-
hogs and foxes as well
as for bird and bat species,
who are totally dependent
on them. Insects are the
balance keepers, being
natural predators of
food crop decimators like
aphids. They also work hard in
the decomposition process to keep our soil alive and rich
in nutrients.

There are so many weird and wonderful types of insects,
including butterflies and moths and their
larvae, worms, wasps and bees, slugs
and snails, beetles, centipedes, spiders, and all sorts of grubs and teeny
tiny creatures. Creating habitats in
our ARKs for the millions of different species of insects would
be nigh on impossible, but one

thing they all have in common is their relationship to native plants. They either eat native plants, eat other insects who eat those plants, or are parasites on other creatures that eat the plants.

Insects are often plant specific and are dependent on a native plant ecosystem being in place, as these plants have evolved within the context of their local food web. We know so little about these intricate relationships that the best support we can give insects is to have as diverse a native plant range in our ARKs as possible. Insects can't thrive without the wild and native weeds and plants, and those plants can't survive without insects pollinating them. Blindly and unfortunately, we are not leaving room for either to survive. We have forgotten they are our gods, deities to be honoured and thanked every single day.

Following are descriptions of a few projects to support insects in your ARK.

A SUMMARY OF
INSECT-SUPPORTING IDEAS

❁ Grow native plants.

❁ Allow dead plant material to accumulate in your garden. Let layers of leaves and twigs rot on the ground, and leave dead wood and log piles.

❁ Build dead hedges, a fantastic tool in any ARK, creating an instant windbreak and a wonderful insect habitat, which also offers happy foraging for birds.

❁ Collect rock piles or put up dry stone walls, a great home of choice for the small creatures.

❁ Provide ponds, both ephemeral and permanent, with shallow areas of water, and rocks and twigs breaking the surface and connecting to the "mainland" to allow them safe spots to live and drink without drowning.

❁ Grow long grass and meadows.

Bee and bug hotels

If done properly, bee and bug hotels are a great way to encourage a range of insects and are easy and fun to make. Actually, the best practice is to allow hollow stems to stand over the winter and be left in piles when you do cut them, but until your ARK is providing these habitats naturally, it might be fun to make one. Some of the shop-bought ones are useless, not deep enough and full of dodgy chemicals. Better to make your own, stacking deadwood and hollow stems from your winter garden inside a wooden frame, providing lots of nooks and crannies and safe, dark winter homes. Use a mixture of tubes, like bamboo, reeds, dead stems of your wild plants like dock, or dead stems from your herb and vegetable patch like fennel, teasel, or lovage.

These replicate the homes that will become more and more naturally available to your mini beasts as your ARK develops and the range and types of deadwood increase. Pinecones, twigs, dead grass, and bits of bark are useful homes, too, as are old bricks with holes in them and dry leaves, which mimic the woodland floor. You could also drill a few holes in the face of some small fresh logs, making sure the holes are deeper than 6 inches (15 centimetres).

Lacewings and ladybirds, solitary bees and wasps, woodlice, and many more creatures will appreciate the safety and existence of suitable hibernation places.

Here are some rules to make sure bee and bug hotels are positive supports:

* ❋ Make the structure small, no bigger than a yard (metre) high. Big hotels are much less likely to be healthy, and if a virus or parasite strikes, all the residents will get infected. If you are really enthusiastic, perhaps make more than one small one and place them in various locations.

* ❋ Divide the hotel into sections and stuff each section with different natural materials, which will allow the house to breathe. Use a wide variety of materials and be sure the twig and stem holes range from a tenth to a third of an inch (2 to 10 millimetres) in diameter. Don't use man-made materials like plastic.

* ❋ Make sure the nesting tubes are a minimum of 6 inches (15 centimetres) long. Bamboo stems that

are sectioned off by inner walls can be too short to use. Nesting tubes should be sealed at the back so that parasites can't gain easy access. Mason bees use mud to do this. You can try the same trick or cover the back with a sheet of wood.

✺ The roof of the structure needs to be waterproof and to overhang sufficiently to protect the home from rain. Moisture will cause the larvae to rot.

✺ Place the hotel in a sunny spot at least 4 feet (1.2 metres) above the ground. Maybe you could attach it to the side of your house, making use of your own eaves to help protect the small creatures in the structure.

✺ It is vital to clean out bug hotels or make fresh ones every year. Otherwise, parasites could build up. This is the reason most commercial bee hotels are a disaster. Sadly, in many shop-bought bee and bug hotels, the nesting materials are glued into place, so they cannot be removed and cleaned. This leads to an explosion of parasites, mites, bacteria, fungi, and viruses attacking the insects you are trying to support.

Wild native bee supports

A quarter of all known bee species have not been seen since 1990, but honeybees seem to get all the attention. Although honeybees are important for agriculture, they also destabilize ecosystems by competing with our native bees for the dwindling food sources. And the wild plants are the food sources that are dwindling the most.

The loss of native-wildflower-rich meadows is cited as having the greatest impact on bee species. Overgrazing on farms is not allowing flowers a chance to grow. Climate collapse is a major problem for bees, too, because their natural habitats, already cut-off islands that are few and far between, are moving location too quickly for the bees to keep up. They can't find the stopover replenishing stations that allow them to move with the habitats.

This is one reason why ARKs will be important. We can create island oases in the green and grey deserts that we have developed so quickly. Our ARKs will be stepping-stones of hope for these gorgeous little creatures.

There are twenty thousand bee species in the world, and only 3 percent of them are the types of bees that live in social colonies. Most of them are solitary bees, and they need support in a variety of nesting situations. Here in Ireland, for example, we have *Osmia aurulenta*, a solitary mason bee who has evolved to nest only in empty snail shells on sand dunes. Other bees make their nests in cavities in stone walls. Some use south-facing banks of bare earth or sand, while some nest aboveground in tufty grasses.

Do some research to find out which bees are native to your own part of the world and what kinds of habitats they might prefer. In our Irish ARKs, we can provide and build patches of the following types of preferred bee homes:

✿ heathland

✿ native flowering meadows

✿ south-facing bare earth banks

✿ sandy banks

✿ dry stone walls

✿ tufty uncut native grasses

✿ standing deadwood or log piles

Beehives for ARKs

Keep a hive simply to offer support to the wild bees that really are beleaguered and under pressure from the non-native honeybees. You don't have to harvest their honey. Our job now is to support nature, not to take more than we need from it. Beehives are available that follow the guidelines of natural beekeeping and are more about bee conservation than honey production. The Natural Beekeeping Trust in England is a great starting point for research on these hives. There are different types, including the egg-shaped Sun Hive and the log hives from Boomtreebees in Ireland.

I have a wild-bee-supporting hive from the wonderful craftsman Mike O'Sullivan in Ireland, trading under the name Let It Beehive 365. Like the Sun Hive, this hive has an excess-honey storage section, which I could harvest if the bees had a huge excess one year without disturbing all their hard work and food store for the coming winter.

After I put this hive in position in my ARK, it was inhabited by a wild native bee colony that my neighbour was called in to remove from somewhere else. I am so glad to support the bees and have them come to stay. The smell of honey wafting out on a sunny day always makes me smile. I sit and tell them all my stories and worries, a traditional practice in these islands, where they are believed to be able to transfer messages to those souls who have passed on. They are the best listeners!

Dung beetle support

Dung beetles are valuable workers in the web of life. They take the dung of animals, tunnel in it, breed in it, pull it down underground, and aerate the soils, recycling the nutrients while reducing greenhouse gas emissions. These beetles are in turn a vital food for many bird and bat species. Sadly, by not joining the dots of the impact of

chemicals, we have almost wiped out our vital dung beetles due to the overuse of worming and parasite treatments
in farm and domestic animals.

According to Dr. Sarah Beynon, who has a research
bug farm in Pembrokeshire, Wales, broadly speaking the
worst killers of dung beetles are the worming drugs with
names that end in -*ectin*, such as ivermectin, moxidectin,
and doramectin. The alternatives that don't kill beetles are
the treatments that are based on chemicals ending in -*ole*,
such as fenbendazole and albendazole, or -*antel*, such as
pyrantel and closantel. But let's face it, these are still bound
to have effects on other creatures. If you have animals to
care for, plenty of alternative treatments are available to try
such as diatomaceous earth, garlic, and homeopathic and
herbal treatments. Using such treatments instead of the
toxic ones, if successful, will protect the beetle populations
in your ARK.

ARK LIGHTING

Artificial lighting is a silent killer of ecosystems. The blue- and white-toned LED lighting now in standard use is a major factor in biodiversity collapse, especially the insect apocalypse that is upon us. Human artificial illumination of the earth is growing by 2 percent a year, causing disruption of natural systems. It is affecting breeding cycles, patterns of activity, hormone levels, and vulnerability to predators. Trees are budding earlier and earlier; seabirds are flying into lighthouses and overlit building exteriors.

Nighttime insects are blinded by LED lights, reducing pollination and breaking important links in the food web for night feeders such as bats. Insects are drawn to fast-moving car lamps, and many of us will remember having to wash clean the car windscreen from dead insects. This isn't necessary these days, as the insect populations have dwindled so much. We seem to keep encouraging them to the road edges with wildflower verges, thinking we are doing a great service to them. It's insulting and can be deadly to them.

At the root of this need to light everything up is the human desire to push back the night. We are still afraid of the dark! I always encourage people to create a nighttime space in their ARKs in the darkest part of their land where they can sit quietly. As your eyes adjust, if you are very quiet, you will see a whole world of creatures emerge in the safety of darkness. It is pure magic.

The solutions to deadly artificial lighting are simple.

If you absolutely *must* have outdoor lights, make sure they are switched to a motion-sensor-only system. This way, they come on only for short times when you need them and allow darkness to prevail in between.

Please make sure all your necessary outdoor *and* indoor bulbs are amber or red in tone. These tones don't affect creatures nearly as much as the blue- and white-toned LEDs that blind them and cause most of the problems. Red is always the safest choice, as amber tones sometimes blind creatures such as fireflies in some parts of the world.

At Christmas, use red-toned bulbs if you want to light up your house or any trees outside, not the blue- or white-toned ones. The trees and their creatures hate the blue- and white-toned ones—not that they are crazy about any of them.

If you are plagued by those commonly used LED street-lights lighting up your urban ARK, write to your local government explaining the issue and asking for support to change the bulbs to amber or red tones, or ask whether filters can be retrofitted over the existing bulbs. More and more good people are emerging in every organization, so you will be surprised at the help and support you will find if you ask.

The Kingdoms Beneath Our Feet

The biggest ecosystem in the whole world is living beneath our feet. The microbial realm in this vast world is invisible to the naked eye. A teaspoon of healthy soil contains more bacteria than there are people on the earth. One square foot of healthy soil has thousands of miles of mycelia, the threadlike roots of fungi, which are the earth's underground World Wide Web communication network. Soil organisms living underground play roles in soil aeration, nutrient cycling, and soil water uptake, which make possible the healthy establishment of plants.

Fungi

Fungi are vital components of the web of life, and they are found everywhere in large numbers—in the air, the seas, the rivers, the soil, and our bodies. Many different types of fungi have been identified. Some are vital decomposition specialists, known as "the teeth of the forest" (saprotrophs), returning organic material back to the earth and thus completing the circle of life. Others called mycorrhizae form a relationship with the roots of plants in which both parties get their needs for nutrition met. Fungi partner with bacteria to carry out this work.

Mycorrhizal fungi have symbiotic relationships with roughly 90 percent of all plants, with some plant roots having more than a hundred species of fungi attached. These fungi attach to the roots of plants through tiny threads called hyphae and feed on the carbohydrates that plants make through photosynthesis. In return, the fungi hold the soil together, protect the plants from disease, and transport nutrients from the soil to the plants or between plants. These are nutrients that bacteria have unlocked and that are moved along the mycelia threads between plants on their orders.

Field mushrooms in Ireland are the fruits of the underground fungal root system. We used to collect buckets of them for teatime when we were small. My dad would fry them and put a knob of butter and a sprinkle of salt on them. Delicious—but sadly, they haven't appeared on this land since I was young.

Fungi connect the whole world together, but we have broken these links belowground by our treatment of topsoil. Routine spraying of chemical fungicides and consistent application of petroleum-based fertilizers in agriculture are burning the fungi out of existence. Concrete and tarmac roads and footpaths, industrial estates, heavy machinery, and urban sprawl compact the soil and isolate the plants from the fungal network of nutrient transportation and their access to water. Tilling, ploughing, and digging the soil overexposes it to oxygen, killing off the ecosystem beneath our feet.

Not digging your soil to grow your food goes against all the traditional gardening advice, but it is clear to me that "no-dig" is a much better practice for building nutrition in our food—and a lot less work to boot. This is a simple method of growing food by creating a rich growing environment above the soil, thus protecting the soil life from disruption. More on this in the next chapter.

Bacteria

Bacteria are among our planet's most vital organisms. Our culture tends to believe that there are good bacteria and bad bacteria, but that is a limited perspective. All bacteria serve an essential function—and almost always in a symbiotic partnership with other life forms.

Plants and microbes together are one being. You may be aware that bacteria thrive around the fine root structures of trees and plants, but more recently it has been shown that microbes cover every square centimetre of plant surface above and below the ground. There they participate in a two-way relationship, the plants giving energy (sugars) in exchange for protection and processing services. Because most plants can't move around, they are especially reliant on these partnerships with microbes to help them get essential nutrients.

Microbes are key to managing the pH (protection) on all surfaces, including the soil around root systems, and in breaking down insoluble nutrients to make them available. They are also responsible for the absorption or fixing of nitrogen from the atmosphere and providing it to the plant at the rate required for its optimal growth. Diverse bacterial colonies provide these services not only in plants with root nodules but also on their branches. Bacteria are nature's factories and armies that are unseen to our naked eye.

In these ways and countless others, microbes are an essential link in the network of all life surrounding healthy plants—their ecosystems, including fungi and earthworms, butterflies and predators, and all the rest.

Science has many times witnessed how the bacterial kingdom communicates and cooperates in times of great crisis. Take, for example, nature's response to some of the massive oil spills of the past fifty years. At first the oil spill runs rampant and does enormous damage, with nothing to check its spread. In this period, the oil smothers and kills the native bacteria and everything else in its path. Then at some point some of the local bacteria begin to transmute into bacteria with the ability to digest oil, and these new colonies begin to grow until they are numerous enough to handle and reverse the outside attack.

Some scientists believe these new capabilities are communicated from other bacteria elsewhere in response to an SOS-type message. Regardless of how the defence happens, you can see that bacteria provide a first line of protection against imbalance, infections, and attack. If we could destroy *all* bacteria, we could destroy the foundation of life. Obviously, humans have attempted this strategy in failed programs to control our environment.

Now is the time for a new strategy, and ARKing and rewilding are important components and solutions. In our ARKs we aim to allow the native microorganisms to find balance and evolve symbiotic relationships. In this manner our ARKs and their colonies become a living network of microorganism repositories—like an immune system that is nature's defence against future attacks.

Supports for our invisible friends

Soil is distinguished from dirt by the presence of organic matter and the microorganisms that make up the vast soil ecosystem. Microbes are what support life, and without them you have a dead substrate. This is often the case in urban situations, as developers remove the soil when houses are being built and leave the residents with damaged subsoil.

There are lots of ways of restoring fungi and bacteria to your soil. For a great homemade reboot, you can make microbial compost teas from old undisturbed local soil, where the microbiome is still intact. For example, you can use a handful of undisturbed mulchy soil from under old trees. Some great compost tea recipes can be found on the web if you are not familiar. Or you can buy a selection of native bacteria to add to water and sprinkle over your soil.

To help the tiny and invisible creatures, leave things be. The number one rule of ARKing, remember, is that *no* chemical poisons or fertilizers should be used. Do not dig the earth. Let the underground ecosystem rest and recover. Mulch around any newly planted trees or shrubs with dead plant material such as bark mulch and prunings. Leaving deadwood and leaves to rot in place is a requirement for the survival of so many creatures.

Tiny pockets of rainwater in hollow tree stumps and decaying wood crevices are habitats for a myriad of microorganisms. Even if you can't see them, these mini life forms need help too. You can help them by creating habitats for them, like ephemeral mini log ponds similar to the ones that would naturally form in a working woodland ecosystem. Letting leaves collect in there helps also. This supports bacteria and fungi that break leaves down and turn them back into the earth.

Grow Your Own Food!

The current systems we depend on to produce our food are cracked, in every sense of the word. Many societies gave up growing their own food. Thereafter, land was only assigned value if it was considered pretty or beautiful, and lawns became a way to advertise lives of wealth and ease. The systems of food production that evolved instead have become the driving force behind the collapse of the web of life on this earth. One solution involves stepping outside of the industrial food system, if you are able, and working with some of your land to produce your own healthy food within a balanced, self-sustaining ecosystem, your ARK. If you cannot do this, then support alternative, small-scale, organic and regenerative local food producers.

The Nutty Food System

Industrial farming and fishing and their global fossil-fuel-driven production processes are driving the sixth mass extinction of life on this planet. Our earth just can't continue to feed almost eight billion meat- and fish-eating humans. We are killing more than sixty billion animals every year in a cruel and destructive industry that contributes more greenhouse gases to the atmosphere than all transportation combined.

Almost half of our earth's habitable land has been converted for agricultural use, and up to 70 percent of this is industrially farmed; yet, 70 to 80 percent of the world's food is produced by small family farmers using organic, permaculture, agroecological, and traditional mixed farming systems. Go figure.

Although 60 percent of the world's agricultural land is used to grow crops to feed cattle, beef accounts for only 2 percent of all calories consumed by humans. There is a huge opportunity here to restore a lot of land to nature and protect our life-giving ecosystems. Imagine the almost-instant effects if we stopped eating grain-fed cattle and started growing healthy food in less cruel and destructive ways, on a much smaller amount of land.

However, changing over to a plant-based diet won't solve everything if it is still dependent on chemical-heavy monocultures. We can't buy our way out of this crisis. We have to face the truth of our broken systems and go back to living in harmony with our shared kin on this earth body of ours.

In Ireland, where the small farmers are rapidly being sidelined out of their professions by Big Agriculture, we are, bizarrely, net food importers, a totally insane position for a country with a terrible history of famine, with land that has some of the most fertile soil on the planet and where crops are easy to grow. It is indicative of the collapse in common sense.

Change from the Ground Up

It is not the farmers who are to blame; it is the system they are caught in. In the absence of any strong political will to change this system, it will only change from the ground up, at least initially, from the efforts of individual farmers, and they need our support to change. Every country has different situations and solutions, but the solutions do exist. Paul Hawken's book *Regeneration: Ending the Climate Crisis in One Generation* has all the solutions in one packet and is an invaluable resource that every political leader should be forced to read.

The worn-out, widely quoted question that is always thrown out when the current food system is queried is:

How will we feed the world without industrially driven, chemical-heavy farming? My answer is always: by supporting people to feed themselves! This is not a profit-laden solution, so it is always ignored. On top of that, in the current system, most people cannot (or think they cannot) afford healthy food. Sadly, large urban areas have vast food deserts where people can't get real food unless they have lots of money or have access to a garden or an allotment and are growing it themselves. Ron Finley ("The Gangsta Gardener") in Los Angeles is tackling the urban deserts by educating people on food issues from the ground up.

One way for an individual to change the destructive system is to stop supporting it. If you have any land under your care, work with some of it to grow chemical-free food if you are able. It's incredible how much food you can grow in a small space. If for any reason you can't manage this, see

FOOD PIONEERS
AND HEROES

Wonderful people are emerging with food system solutions, and these people are usually in need of support themselves. It's not easy to be a trailblazer, to be forging new paths, to step outside the system in order to create a new one. It's usually a financial vacuum, and it takes a lot of courage to throw yourself over that particular cliff.

In Ireland, the organization Farming for Nature (FFN) is in the vanguard of the new growing movement, driving the positive narrative that farmers can be part of the solution to our mounting climate and biodiversity crisis, with many wonderful examples. FFN understands that farmers are potentially a huge resource in responding to the crisis. It celebrates the farmers already doing great things for nature and also advocates strongly for farmers to be supported financially to deliver ecosystem services on their farms. Also in Ireland, Talamh Beo is a grassroots, farmer-led organization that aims to ensure a living landscape where people and ecosystems can thrive together.

Also check out Rebecca Hosking and Agriwilding in the UK, Farmer's Footprint in the US, Ecosystem Restoration

Camps, and the many wonderful agroforestry and permaculture experts. Geoff Lawton is one of my heroes in Australia; his permaculture research institute with its farm is a beacon of light in the world.

Amber Tamm is one powerhouse based in New York. She is fighting to establish a food farm in Central Park to promote food sovereignty. Amber is a farmer without her own land, highlighting the racial injustices and lack of access to land faced especially by young and minority farmers. Sandra Salazar D'eca is the founder of Go Grow with Love, working to teach children in London to grow food using traditional and Indigenous ways, and connecting city folk with mother nature.

These are just a few of the many true leaders emerging in the world of food farming and gardening, all of them teaching wisdom and empowerment. Research your local food pioneers and support them if you can.

if you can switch to buying food from local, regenerative, and organic producers. This is an important step toward having a low impact and imprint on the earth.

Buying food that is grown locally is so important, as the practice of transporting food around the planet in massive refrigerated containers is crazy. Organic food grown on one side of the world is shipped halfway around the globe to be processed and wrapped in plastic, only to be transported back again to be distributed into shops. It's simply nuts, and food handled this way cannot be called organic in the true sense of the word.

You may need to do a bit of research to find locally produced, healthy food. These growers are not always online. Search out local farmers markets for sources, organic vegetable box schemes, and local organic CSAs (community supported agriculture organizations). The more support the local producers get, the more likely it is that they can survive and thrive and the weaker the insane global system will become.

Feed the Soil, Feed Your Body

"We need a new definition of malnutrition. Malnutrition means under- and over-nutrition. Malnutrition means emaciated and obese." So wrote Catherine Bertini, executive director of the United Nations World Food Programme from 1992 to 2002.

These days, obesity kills more people than famine. Both situations are completely and tragically unnecessary. When the soil is healthy, so is the food, but nowadays we must deal with the "dilution effect" in our food. As a result of our constant exploitation of the soil, we are removing minerals faster than the soil can replenish them. Most conventional food crops are dependent on the addition of synthetic fertilizers to grow, but only three nutrients are traditionally added to get the crops up and out of the ground: potassium, nitrogen, and phosphorus (NPK), all derived from petrochemicals. Recently many farmers are adding a few extra minerals to the mix, but these few do not stack up against the complex range of hundreds of macro- and micronutrients our bodies need in order to be healthy.

Since 1950, the vitamin and mineral content of our food has dropped considerably. The average mineral content has fallen by 85 percent in the United States and 76 percent in Asia. Our immune systems are really compromised by poor nutrition. "You are what you eat," as the saying goes.

Higher yield has been the holy grail for farming, but it comes at a cost. One relevant study showed that applying high levels of phosphorous to a crop of raspberries doubled the yield but conversely caused a 20- to 55-percent drop in the levels of eight other vital minerals within the produce. There is also evidence of a decline in plant nutrition that goes hand in hand with breeding crops for higher yields. The hardier and healthier plants are, the greater resistance to disease they have. Like ours, their health is based on their diet.

We must start feeding the soil again so that we can feed our bodies properly. What we do to the earth is directly reflected in the state of our health.

Her health is ours. Our lives are hers.

Organically produced food does contain more nutrition, as those farmers use animal manures and composts filled with microbes to grow their crops rather than adding the conventional petrochemical-based NPK. However, organic farming on a large scale is not a complete solution. Regenerative and permaculture-based solutions need to be incorporated to restore and protect the soil.

The soil in your garden is likely to be in better shape than agricultural land but will benefit from the addition of natural minerals and organic matter. Most of us are aware by now that adding organic material back into the soil is vital for soil health. The benefits of adding compost and animal manures to the soil have been well documented. But we also need to replace the inorganic material, the minerals. Ecosystems can develop much faster when missing minerals are restored.

There are a few methods of remineralizing the soil, including biochar, seaweed, and mineral rock dust.

Biochar is a high-carbon form of charcoal created by heating organic matter at very high temperatures in the absence of oxygen. Farmers have been using it for centuries to improve soil. It adds structure that supports a healthy aerobic underground ecosystem, leading to improved plant nutrition and health. You can obtain biochar online, but make sure it is responsibly sourced and has a traceable origin. Follow the manufacturer's instructions. In general, you can simply sprinkle it on top of your soil and wet it, but the best practice involves activating it first by burying it in your compost heap for a couple of weeks. The biochar will soak up nutrients and microbes from the compost, later releasing them slowly wherever you spread it around your ARK.

Seaweed added to your growing beds can also restore the missing minerals to your food and your body. You can collect washed-up seaweed by hand if you live near the ocean, although there may be laws in your part of the world that restrict seaweed collection, so it is best to check first. Even if not illegal, overharvesting of seaweed is a serious issue for ocean ecosystems, so you need to be very careful not to take too much. In early Ireland, the native law system called the Brehon Laws stipulated that only one-seventh of a plant (or other foraged things) should be taken, no more. It is still a good number to work with. You can also purchase hand-harvested seaweed dust for this purpose.

Rock dust is a by-product of the rock-grinding processes carried out in quarries. You can download a brilliant and simple guide to this method from remineralize.org, explaining what types of rock dust to use, how much, and when. This dust can be spread on your ARK and growing beds in the spring or autumn or can be incorporated into the compost heap before adding the compost to the growing beds.

Restoring to the soil the minerals and organic matter with their accompanying microorganisms is an important start. Not tilling or digging your soil is also important. We have been taught for years that tilling or digging is the way to access fertile soil. In truth, digging results in an initial burst of fertility but soon leads to the die-off of the soil microbial ecosystem from overexposure to oxygen. The soil becomes less and less alive every time you do this, forcing you to add fertility from the top down. This does help the food to grow, but it is not nutrient-rich food with the full range of micronutrients.

Practices for Food Self-Sufficiency

Small-scale, home-grown production methods based on permaculture and the no-dig method are the way forward, in my opinion.

COMPOST YOUR LEFTOVER FOOD

If you throw food in the general waste bin, it goes to a landfill. A lack of oxygen in landfills, necessary in the decomposition of organic wastes, results in the production of methane, a gas that is twenty times more destructive to the atmosphere than carbon dioxide when it is released. Instead, put those nutrients right back into the soil system if you can. Generally, it's suggested you put raw, plant-based food into a compost bin and cooked food into a wormery or a hot compost bin.

More and more community composting schemes are popping up, and if you live in an apartment you may be able to contribute to one. If you are lucky enough to have room for some chickens, kitchen scraps are easily redistributed as tasty snacks, which get processed into the best fertilizer that comes out the other side!

In simple terms, no-dig gardening is a way to grow food without breaking your back or damaging the soil ecosystem. You will need a large amount of peat-free compost for this method, but once you have that sorted, it's an easy way to build a vegetable garden. Begin with some lawn or other undug ground in the garden (as long as it is not badly compacted) and cut back the existing plant growth to the ground. Then put down multiple layers of cardboard, poke holes through it, wet it, and cover it with at least 6 inches of peat-free compost. Plant your vegetable seeds or little food plants grown from seed directly into this. It's all about feeding and protecting the soil so that we can grow nutrient-rich food. Every year, apply more well-rotted manure or compost to the beds. To protect the soil in fallow periods, you can use cover crops that are then chopped back and mulched over to prepare for new plantings.

Permaculture is a term coined from *permanent agriculture*. It revolves around developing systems of settlement and agriculture that incorporate and learn from the interconnections and relationships of natural ecosystems. It draws from many layers of sustainable practices such as agroforestry, ecology, organic farming, and sustainable development. Permaculture is guided by three design principles: care for people, care for the earth, and careful process that means everyone gets their fair share.

I love permaculture concepts like forest gardening, which involves growing perennial plants in multiple layers in an open-canopy, productive woodland. Combined with native plants, this is a magical way of working with land, modeled on nature's own systems. Basically, it involves growing perennial food plants in seven layers on the same piece of land, mimicking a forest ecosystem. The layers are canopy trees, understory trees, shrubs, perennials, ground covers, underground plants like root vegetables and fungi, and climbers or vines. You can put in as many or as few layers as you have room for.

Forest gardening involves careful planning to keep enough space between the plants to allow sufficient light. ARKevists in some parts of the world will need to plan for more shade than light, whereas in places like Ireland these systems need to be kept quite open to be successful, with the low level of light we have here. Forest gardens can take many years and a lot of work to develop and become abundant, but abundant they do become. There are huge resources on the web and multiple books out there on the different forest garden plants for each unique region of the world.

Planting with the future in mind is also important. In a heating world, certain crops will be more resilient in different regions. Lots of resources are beginning to come out about this subject, so do some research about the plants that will do well in the future in your own area.

Polytunnels or glasshouses are very helpful in many climates to help a family become food self-sufficient. Plastic isn't the best, of course, but weighing it up, I feel it makes sense if it allows you to step out of the current system. It's certainly a better option than buying plastic-wrapped organic food from faraway shores. However, if you *can* afford a glasshouse, go for it.

SEEDS ARE SACRED

One of the scariest things happening these days is the insidious corporate takeover of our precious seeds. Corporations are trying (and succeeding) to patent them, modify them, and create profits by controlling the access to seeds for food—the ultimate control. As Henry Kissinger said, "Control oil and you control nations; control food and you control the people."

Resist this at all costs! Do not go buying seeds unconsciously from a garden centre or a supermarket. Grow only from organic heritage seeds and locally sourced open-pollinated seed, and learn how to save your own seed every year. Support small organic seed companies and organizations such as Seed Savers Exchange in the US, Irish Seed Savers, and Brown Envelope Seeds in Ireland. With a little research, you will find similar small seed savers in your own part of the world.

Share and Create a Community

If you have a large garden and restore half of it into an ARK, the remaining half I'm suggesting you use for food growing may be very large. So why not consider sharing some of the space to grow food with as many friends as possible? Many urban dwellers have no gardens.

Alternatively, if you don't have a garden and need to grow food, perhaps you could approach an elderly friend who has a garden but not the health to work with it. In exchange for working with their land to build an ARK and grow food, you could share the produce and enrich their lives greatly. Often older people are terribly lonely, and this would be such a gift, to have some company and the interest of watching out for the many wild creatures that will inevitably arrive to share in their patch of earth. Share plants, knowledge, and food, and just help each other. Give your life and theirs some meaning, belonging, and warmth.

Community allotments are so important for urban dwellers, we need to lobby for more and more land for this purpose. There's room in the ARK community for everyone!

Wider ARKevism

One person can create big changes through the ripple effect of inspiration, so never feel your efforts are in vain. People are always motivated by the positive actions of others. To have a broader impact on the world, connect with our ARKevist community through the We Are the ARK Facebook group. Create a local ARK group where you can share seeds and cuttings, have sign-making workshops, and help each other with knowledge and support. With your group or alone, you might want to lobby local and national officials to take on ARKing projects and aims.

For example, you could tackle your local government or council to resolve the problems caused by blue- and white-toned streetlights in urban areas, a lack of wildlife road crossings, and such. Look around you and consider where the opportunities for change are. I will list some more ideas in the following pages. Just remember not to browbeat or lecture anyone, as that shuts down their hearts and ears. It is always best to inspire change through positive action and setting an example, which shows people that things can be different and encourages them to see their input and efforts as important. Empowerment is the aim.

With the realization that everything must change, many inventive and resourceful people will be willing to take on the challenges we face and turn them into opportunities. The solutions are out there. We just need to embrace them, quickly. An exciting new world awaits.

ARKs on School, Public, and Commercial Lands

Why would anyone responsible for school, public, or commercial lands want to jump on board the ARK project?

There is a growing wave of awareness worldwide that we need to change our land-use policies, expediently become more supportive of nature, and embrace a green future with local strategies. By rewilding free open spaces at schools, derelict land, industrial estates, and large areas of parks that are unused, local officials can become part of the solution and set an example. Goodwill is the harvest from joining up with this ARK rewilding concept. Plus marking out areas as ARKs reduces the maintenance costs incurred to keep everything neat and tidy.

In short, ARKing is a positive movement for local officials to attach themselves to, one that grows their green image, requires very little input, and reduces their costs. It's a triple-win situation!

Keys to a successful public ARK

To make a public ARK successful, the main key is to involve the local community. Putting local people at the heart of these projects means the ARK will have constant custodians and carers, ensuring its success.

Then select the right places for the ARK and don't go planting the wrong plants in the wrong place (if planting is even needed). Research the land in question. Work with an ecologist and search out local knowledge of what the land used to be clothed with. That will become the baseline aim for your restoration project.

Use natural regeneration wherever you can, removing the non-natives that may have found their way in there and giving the weed-seed bank time to emerge. These natural ARKs will be the most diverse, will cost the least, and will be the most resilient, as the native seeds will be adapted to local conditions. If, however, the land is poisoned or damaged, remove the non-native species and follow the steps set out in this book to restore health and diversity to it.

Remember to put up a sign saying "This is an ARK" to explain what is happening so that you are not accused of the usual concerns of neglect or laziness.

Potential places for ARKs

Think of all those places that could be pulled in under the umbrella of an ARK! Here are some examples:

* Sports clubs. Every sports club (soccer club, rugby club, tennis club; in Ireland, GAA club) has the potential to be more representative of the community than any government could ever be. These clubs have huge influence within grassroots communities and could be a powerful inspiration with very little effort, leading by example, by turning unused land into an ARK and community allotments.

* Public parks. These have so many areas that are not used, patches that could become ARKs and reduce the need for maintenance while earning a lot of admirers. Parks departments could also aim to

populate public landscapes with only native plants, a simple but powerful change.

✿ Those countless mown island beds and shrubbery borders around every office building and shopping centre. Bring them back to life and create habitats for life.

✿ Industrial estates. These are usually ugly concrete jungles. Their footprints on the land beneath and around them could be offset a little by restoring a simple native ecosystem to those small places within them that are not covered by concrete.

✿ Disused railway lines.

Roadsides might be thought of as a possibility, but I am not a fan of roadside ARKs. These make wildlife very vulnerable to death or injury from the lethal machines zooming past them constantly. Please don't put creatures in harm's way. Would you want to live next to a motorway? We keep cutting them off from their territories and food sources, making their island homes smaller and smaller, allocating our unusable and dangerous spaces as wildlife zones. *Greenwashing* is the only term for it. This has got to stop and needs to be retrospectively remedied. They deserve better choices.

The solution is simple. Supplying wildlife bridges and tunnels across and underneath roads, with solid fences stopping creatures from crossing unsafely elsewhere, would be a wonderful way of supporting the understanding that we are only sharing this planet. Every county development plan and road-building scheme should be forced by law to embrace these additions to their construction. It's only right, when you realize how dependent we are on nature's web of life staying intact and healthy. You can't put a price on our survival as a species.

Schools are also often potential sites for ARKs. Educating youngsters about the state of nature and the necessary solutions is so important. Unless children are given an opportunity to get to know the natural world, how will they understand what is happening to it? How will they protect what they do not know or love?

School grounds may have spaces where ARKs can be shared. Nest boxes with cameras and night vision wildlife cameras connected to active screens in the school communal areas are great ways to engage the kids. The most important key is to get them to develop the ARKs themselves, to feel a real connection with these places, watch the ecosystems develop, learn about their native plants, and discover the magical creatures that share even the smallest spaces, if we let them.

Political ARKevism

Most of this work involves lobbying your local and national politicians to change policies relating to cracked rules. Education is key, and if that doesn't work, old and entrenched policy makers need to be replaced quickly. This is a matter of our survival as a species, and if they are not getting that, they must give way to others who have vision and courage. The science is clear on this. We are running out of time, fast.

Rewild our oceans

We have got to step up and become protectors of the seas as well as the land. Rewilding at least half of our oceans is a vital part of our recovery. However, we are rapidly emptying the seas of all life. Restoring mangrove forests, seaweed and seagrass colonies, kelp forests, and coral reefs is going to be a major part of the action plan to ensure we have a future on this planet.

Encourage the politicians to support small fishing businesses and traditional family fishing concerns as part of the necessary move away from industrial fishing. As mentioned earlier in the book, bottom trawling fishing practices are catastrophic and must stop immediately. Giving back fishing rights to local coastal communities with low-impact fishing traditions is also going to be important. The consequent restored vibrant sea ecosystems will create more economic stability and lateral opportunities for many communities around the world.

Governments everywhere must cease their insane war against our ocean creatures in the form of sanctioned seismic surveys by oil and gas companies. These surveys use sound pressure waves—loud pulses that are 100,000 times louder than a jet engine and can be heard 1,800 miles (3,000 km) away—to detect gas and oil deposits. Because whales and dolphins rely on sound to hunt, navigate, and communicate, these sonar pulses lead to mass groundings and deaths of our beautiful sea giants. This noise pollution impacts every single organism in the marine ecosystem and even causes large-scale die-off of zooplankton.

Great people are working hard to counteract all this insanity. All over the world, coral reefs are being reseeded, mangroves are being planted along coasts, and kelp forests are being protected by local people from the greed of politically backed corporations.

Restore our wetlands

Support your local government to restore wetlands. Wetlands are among the most valuable ecosystems, creating a wide range of specialized habitats and also sequestering carbon. In the past three hundred years, 87 percent of the world's wetlands have been destroyed or lost–a third of that number since the 1970s, when industrial agriculture ramped up its intensification.

Peatlands, a type of wetland ecosystem, come in two main types called bogs and fens. Fens are peatlands that are fed by underground and surface water, whereas bogs are mostly fed by rainwater. Mosses grow abundantly in these waterlogged conditions, creating microhabitats that thousands of unique creatures of all kinds–including many rare birds, plants, and insects–are dependent upon for survival.

The presence and health of our wetlands is directly connected to the severity of flooding, as they are responsible for regulating water flow. Wetlands are nature's sponges. No wonder flooding is such a problem. Of course, widespread tree removal is also a major issue, as mature trees can drink up to 50 gallons (190 litres) of water every day and the roots of trees draw water down deep into the earth, holding the water system steady.

Let floodplains flood

If your ARK is in a natural floodplain, you can be sure it is an abundant and important habitat.

Many of the current solutions imposed by flood management programs do not consider the effects on the natural world. Blocking floodplains off from rivers by replacing the banks with big vertical concrete walls destroys habitats, acting like a guillotine. It has been commonplace in building and farming to drain floodplains completely to allow more development, but this only causes bigger problems downstream and removes many creatures from their rightful homes.

It's time to take a step "backward" and allow rivers to roll along at their own pace and breathe, to be absorbed into the earth during periods of high rainfall in ephemeral floodplain wetlands, natural overflow areas designed to slow the waters down. A specialist ecosystem has developed over the ages in these wetlands, and we need them to be the great big sponges they are.

Extreme flood events, outside the normal range of floodplain expansion, are one of the results of the climate collapse we are already experiencing. These events are terribly destructive to an ecosystem, introducing more pollutants, agricultural soil, and organic matter into the system. Erosion is increased dramatically and populations of plants, invertebrates, and vertebrates are severely impacted instantly. The ability of an ecosystem to recover from these events is low. The only way resilience to these extreme events is achieved is by improving habitat connections in our waterside sponges and by providing safe-haven refuges that can be used during flood events.

Let rivers meander

Raise your voice to educate your local councils and farmers to halt the widespread, dreadful dredging and straightening policies that are destroying rivers all over. Speeding up the flow of rivers to get rid of the water more quickly is not a solution. We actually need to slow it down, allow it time to be processed, time to soak into the earth. Otherwise we are just causing bigger flooding problems downstream.

Support farmers to work with nature

Ask your politicians to change policy to support local farmers to work with nature. At the moment, they are often penalized for allowing natural areas to develop or for not following the destructive rules and policies they must adhere to in order to receive financial aid. It would help farmers to be supported to think outside the box in the following ways:

✿ Encourage farmers to change farming practices to no-till, chemical-free agroforestry, regenerative, and permaculture systems, and to rewild wide sections of farms that run alongside river courses. Restoring native hedgerows—increasing the number of years between cuts and allowing them to grow broad and tall—creates habitats and corridors that are invaluable to wildlife.

✻ Support farmers to build upstream ephemeral ponds and swales (ditches dug on level contour lines) to hold runoff water longer. Local landowners need to be encouraged to work with ecologists to restore original watercourse patterns to stabilize riverbanks, reboot ecosystems, and slow down water.

✻ Pay farmers to rewild the uplands. Currently the uplands are often used as unprofitable sheep ranches (a major problem in Ireland and the UK) and some are kept bare by wild goats and deer. These grazers, being so out of balance in their numbers, eat any young shoots that try to emerge in nature's regenerative processes. Having a policy in place to compensate farmers to erect suitable fencing to keep the grazers away from the uplands and allow natural regeneration to take place would solve problems and create opportunities. Typically the land would quickly revert to vast, restored

native woodland systems that would become wildlife refuges large and healthy enough to reintro-
duce apex predators. This would create ecotourism
possibilities and other possible prospects for farmers. Restored upland woodlands would also slow
down the flow of water and stabilize the system
downstream. Currently, over here in Ireland, farmers have their farm payments docked if any areas of
land are left "unfarmed"–a truly crazy system that
causes a rift between farmers and the environmen-
talists who don't understand the financial stresses
on the landowners.

Some land may need support to restore its ecosystems
by planting intermittently with pockets of locally sourced
native trees. Alan Watson Featherstone's Trees for Life
project in Scotland is a wonderful example of this process.
Another of my great heroes, Rebecca Hosking, is a trailblazer with her wonderful agriwilding practices on her
farm in England. Her eight principles of agriwilding take
regenerative farming to a new level, treating each farm as a
shared ecosystem. Two true leaders in our world.

Plan for nature in cities

We can lobby local governments to design development
plans with nature in mind. Lots of native trees, orchards,
and food forests can be incorporated. Poisoned soils can
be remediated, and as much sealed soil (soil locked under
concrete or asphalt) can be released as possible.

Rainwater gardens can be created throughout cities.
These gardens—slight depressions in the earth made at the
base of a natural slope that are then supported to become
an ARK or fully planted with native plants—can get rid of
up to 90 percent of chemicals and nutrients, and 80 percent of sediment runoff. Rainwater gardens can be long,
plant-filled channels in designated green areas below and
running alongside roads and paths, or just sunken beds
placed to catch, hold, and soak away the rain running off
from paths, driveways, roads, and roofs.

Treat sewage naturally

According to the United Nations, a good 80 percent of
wastewater from human activities is pumped back into
nature without being cleaned or treated adequately. We
need to encourage and put pressure on local governments

to change our current sewage treatment systems. Flushing our waste into our water system, pumping it into rivers and seas after a basic "sieve" (as so many places still do), or treating it chemically to turn it back into "drinking water" is wasteful and damaging on many levels to human and ecosystem health. The earth body can handle our waste. The water bodies cannot. Putting the nutrition back into the soil system is the only credible solution.

The current chemical water treatment plants are large and expensive, and they degrade with time. On the other side of the coin, the performance of plant-based treatment systems improves with time. Researchers in Canada have found that more than 30 million litres (almost 8 million gallons) of primary wastewater per hectare (2.47 acres) can be treated annually using short-rotation, coppiced willow beds (based on experiments in Saint-Roch-de-l'Achigan in Quebec). The waste is filtered through the willow roots.

In domestic situations, if people have sufficient land under their care, they should be allowed and supported to have composting toilets and greywater treatment systems. Nature has all the solutions.

THE LIVING MACHINE
AT FINDHORN

In 1995 the Findhorn Ecovillage in Moray, Scotland, installed a wonderful sewage solution called the Living Machine. This was developed by Canadian biologist Dr. John Todd to treat wastewater in a way that mimics the natural purifying mechanisms of wetlands and requires little energy to run. Virtually nothing is wasted in the system because every organism provides food for the next step.

Sewage is first collected in underground tanks that encourage the growth of anaerobic bacteria, among the oldest life forms on Earth and experts at breaking down organic and inorganic matter. Then the wastewater soup flows by gravity to open tanks where microbial communities can flourish and digest particles in the water. Plants with long roots, such as daffodils, are suspended above the tanks, with the roots giving bacteria a place to multiply. The water travels from there through gravel beds where it is subjected to further treatment facilitated by air pumps. Finally, the water is pumped underground to be discharged into nearby sand dunes.

Protect the trees we already have

The highest priority is to protect existing woodlands and rainforests first—*especially* the ancient remnants. These are the most diverse ARKs in existence, and they must be protected at all costs.

Every native tree is an ARK. There is a tendency (particularly here in Ireland, it seems), to brutally flail or roughly cut miles of hedgerows and trees on roadsides and farmland, and to cut down healthy stands of trees in villages, towns, and cities. The neat square and narrow hedgerow is now in fashion, removing all hope of them becoming refuges for nesting or useful as wildlife corridors. It takes thirty years for a tree to become a full-blown oxygen machine. Trees clean our air and water, create shelter and shade, and hold the fast-disappearing soils in place. We should be ashamed at our treatment of and disconnection from these standing elders whose existence allows us to continue living here on Earth.

We need to protect every single tree we have already and plant or allow nature to grow *trillions* more native trees so that we may survive. Make a stand. Step up and protect life. All over the world are living examples of large trees in cities that are appreciated and allowed to become a natural, mature shape. These trees in urban landscapes are hugely beneficial to us, calming anxiety, lifting depression, creating beauty, and sustaining life.

Don't fall for the greenwash narrative that implies that great work is being carried out by planting vast stretches of non-native monocultures. These are not woodlands, they are tree farms—commercial crops. They are usually heavily treated with chemicals to deal with the inevitable pest attacks that overwhelm the imbalanced nature of a monoculture. These stands of tree crops create such dark canopies that almost no life exists beneath them; instead they harbour silence, poison, and damage. Governments regularly try to push this idea of tree farms upon us, as if they are restoring woodland habitats. In reality, it's just more crimes against nature they are encouraging. This idea is not part of the solution to the climate and biodiversity collapse we are facing. Call them out on it. The decision makers at all levels need to become protectors of all life on Earth.

Start with the trees.

Please.

Conclusion: Reimagining Living in Harmony

We live in a magical world filled with miraculous and unbelievable creatures of every possible shape, size, and colour. Some of them are blatantly and ridiculously beautiful—or just plain ridiculous. Have you ever seen a Venezuelan

poodle moth? Or the dance of a superb bird of paradise? Or a narwhal? Seriously, mind-blowing life forms are everywhere. If you look microscopically at the tiny kingdom creatures, they are even more amazing.

Everything you can possibly imagine already exists on this planet we call home. These weird and wonderful creatures must become our reason for being here, to mind them, to provide for them so that they might thrive. We are hopelessly and helplessly dependent on their fragile and interdependent existence.

We are just reflections of the earth; we mirror each other. It is no coincidence that our inner energy is often muted and depressed. All the wild places and wild sanctuaries are being destroyed, and we are in turn becoming bland and empty. But our true natures are wild and magical and are still lingering there beneath the skin, waiting for us to remember.

What a potent word *magic* is. That fizzy, awesome feeling, something children have in abundance and some of us still remember. Magic dies the moment we "grow up" and harden our hearts. It leaves us as soon as we forget that the world is full of mystery and layers of enchantment, seen and unseen. But it returns to us as soon as we restore our connection to the earth and to an awareness of our shared kin.

Magic is eagerly waiting to creep back into your heart as soon as you can crack it open wide enough for your wild nature to return. Once you blend back into the web of life and remember your body is made from the earth and her atmosphere, that all living things that you share this life with are extensions of your own health and happiness, then you step into the flow of magic that connects everything. The sensitivity that returns by regaining the consciousness of those connections reawakens your magical bond with the earth. You can feel the character of each plant, its intention and willingness (or not) to help us. You can sense the malleability of the world, how every thought we have and action we take is a building block for the future we want to create.

We have been living under a spell of our own making. Our imagination, thoughts, emotions, and focus make up our vision, and our vision creates our future lives. Right now, the only visions of the future we are presented with through the media are dystopian images of a dead or dying planet. It's time to imagine and build a beautiful, gentle future. A new vision that allows us to *have* a future.

A restored sense of community, abundance, and peace. A future where we all strive together to support the earth and her life forms to live in health, so that we may continue to live here among them.

It's time to go to work to save the sovereignty of our land, our water, our air, and all the creatures we share this planet with. The earth has become a barren green, brown, and scorched desert, but we can be the ones to create the island oases in this desert. These oases will be the seeding grounds for our new story. They will be sanctuaries for as many creatures as we can fit into them, safe havens for the magic and abundance in the natural world. They will become the ark for the flood of extinction that is already upon us. We are the last frontier and the last generation with enough time left to save this planet, by the skin of our teeth.

One person can effect such big change in this world, simply by inspiring change all around them.

One person, one patch of land, one decision at a time.

Let's dream up that beautiful world we know exists. Each of us is powerful as an individual, but together we are invincible. We have a supportive network here that can counteract the dystopian future we are being offered. Positive imaginings with strong feelings of joy and gratitude attached to them are much more powerful than those heart-breaking visions of a future of extinction and broken dreams.

A gentle approach to life is needed. One where everything is slower, where life has meaning and richness again. Where our neighbours are our support, our communities are our strength, and a simple life becomes one worth living. Where locally grown organic, regenerative, and resilient food systems allow us to step out of a system based on terrible cruelty toward sentient beings and let us give vast amounts of land back to nature so that she can restore her health and grant us a future.

It's time for us human beings to step up and become the weavers of the web of life, to restitch the threads we have broken.

This is a different type of web weaving. It is a web of interconnected life, interconnected magic, and hope.

We are weaving ourselves an ARK.

An Act of Restorative Kindness to the earth.

Appendix:
Getting Started

If you're not sure where to begin, these are some steps you can take right now. Turn to the ARK Design and First Steps chapter for a much more detailed breakdown.

1. Give at least half your garden back to nature. Use the other half to grow your own (organic) food. If you allow your ARK to rewild through nature's natural processes, it will become a more and more complex ecosystem over time. All land is welcome, even a window box full of local soil that allows the native weed seeds to flourish and provide food and reproductive partners for the insects is great.

2. Put up a sign that says, "This is an ARK / wearetheark.org." This simple action will make you proud of your newly wild garden because you're doing something important to help all the creatures we are supposed to share the planet with. Interested neighbours can visit the website to learn more.

3. Remove any non-native "invasive plants." This can be managed easily enough by hand or with borrowed grazers or heavy sheet mulching. Do not use chemicals—there is no place for them in an ARK; they cause many more problems than they solve and are very destructive to life at all levels.

4. You may need to step in and provide some ecosystem services that are lacking due to the absence of the full circle of life. Our goal is to create as many different habitats as possible on our

land, especially those that would otherwise be created by keystone species that are missing from our isolated ARKs. If you have the space, consider the following: meadows, bare-earth banks, piles of deadwood, a pond, a scrubby thorny thicket, a mature native woodland, or a dry-stone wall.

5. Native plants are foundational to all ecosystems. Your ARK should be based on the plants that are native to your region. If your soil is damaged or devoid of growth, the weed-seed bank may be absent. Sow a wildflower meadow to reboot the system and slowly introduce as many native plants as possible. Use only locally sourced native organic seeds, cuttings, and plants, as these provide vital genetic material for the local insect populations and have not been grown with poisons.

6. Create "holes" in your property's boundaries to allow wildlife to pass through. Learn to share your patches of this earth.

7. Examine your ARK's lighting. Standard blue- and white-toned lighting is one of the major contributors to the collapse of biodiversity. Aim for darkness or at least make sure all your ARK lights are red in tone. Make sure all outdoor lights are motion sensor only so that they only come on when you need them and allow darkness to prevail when you don't.

8. Get together with like-minded folk and approach your councils and HOAs, your schools and university campuses, and ask for support to turn more and more park space and public land into ARKs.

9. Mark your ARK on our map of ARKs (wearetheark.org/map-of-arks/). Our hope is to eventually connect these dots, creating more and more wildlife corridors.

References
and Resources

The We Are the ARK website (wearetheark.org) and the We Are the ARK Facebook group are places to connect with the movement and discover resources aside from those listed here. My previous book, *The Garden Awakening: Designs to Nurture Our Land and Ourselves* (Cambridge, England: Green Books, 2016) also offers an alternative way of looking at gardens. It is based around growing a food forest and goes into great detail about how to do it.

The wonderfully talented artist who filled this book with a visual feast is Ruth Evans, ruthevansart.com.

Specific References in the Book

Claire and Joe's Irish Forest Garden (pages 21 and 105), irishforestgarden. ie, grew from my friendship with Claire and her support for *The Garden Awakening* that helped bring it into being.

Doughnut economics (page 44) is described by Kate Raworth in *Doughnut Economics: Seven Ways to Think Like a 21st-Century Economist* (New York: Random House, 2017).

Ecosystem Restoration Camps (pages 82 and 218), ecosystemrestorationcamps.org, is a global movement of people restoring broken ecosystems together.

Greening the Desert Project (page 84), greeningthedesertproject.org, is Australian Geoff Lawton's project in Jordan to provide "living proof that we can reverse desertification and bring back life to desolate barren lands." Lawton teaches permaculture courses through the website, and you can also find his videos of permaculture techniques on YouTube.

Klaus Laitenberger (page 131), *The Self-Sufficient Garden* (Ireland: Milkwood Farm Publishing, 2020), is available at greenvegetableseeds.com.

More information on the "Forest in a Box" project (page 146), as well as a petition to save and expand Ireland's ancient remnant rainforests, can be found at thewoodlandleagueforestinabox.ie.

The Miyawaki method to regenerate native forests (page 150), described at akiramiyawaki.com, was developed by Japanese botanist Akira Miyawaki to create densely planted native forests on small patches of land.

Bird box (page 179) instructions can be found on the websites of the National Trust, nationaltrust.org.uk/features/how-to-make-your-own-bird-box, and the Royal Society for the Protection of Birds (RSPB), rspb.org.uk/birds-and-wildlife/advice/how-you-can-help-birds/nestboxes/nestboxes-for-small-birds/making-and-placing-a-bird-box/.

Bee conservation and education (page 198) information can be found at Natural Beekeeping Trust, naturalbeekeepingtrust.org; Let it Beehive 365, letitbeehive.home.blog/; and Boomtreebees, boomtreebees.com.

Bug research (page 200) is conducted on Dr. Sarah Beynon's Bug Farm, thebugfarm.co.uk, a research centre in Wales that focuses on investigating how we can feed a growing population while still minding our wildlife.

No-dig food production methods (pages 206 and 225) are described in "Beginner's Guide," Charles Dowding website, charlesdowding.co.uk/start-here/; and "The No-Dig Method," Garden Organic website, gardenorganic.org.uk/no-dig-method.

Compost tea (page 209) is explained in "The Best Compost Tea Recipe to Help Your Plants Thrive," by Nicole Faires, learn.eartheasy.com/articles/the-best-compost-tea-recipe-to-help-your-plants-thrive/; and KIS Organics (Redmond, WA), kisorganics.com/pages/simplici-tea, offers compost teas, compost tea brewing systems, and organic bio-amendments.

Food pioneers and heroes (page 218) include Farming for Nature (Ireland), farmingfornature.ie, an initiative that "seeks to acknowledge and support those farmers who farm, or wish to farm, in a way that will improve the natural health of our countryside"; Talamh Beo, talamhbeo.ie, a grassroots, farmer-led Irish organization that aims to ensure a living landscape where people and ecosystems can thrive together; Farmer's Footprint, farmersfootprint.us, video series at youtube.com/farmersfootprint, "Accelerating the universal adoption of regenerative land management for the health of people and the planet"; Amber Tamm, gofundme.com/f/cy4cqn-future-farm-fund; Sandra Salazar D'eca, everydayclimatehero.org/Sandra-salazar-deca; and The Ron Finley Project, ronfinley.com.

Rock dust (page 224) products and instructions are available at remineralize.org.

Heirloom and organic seeds (page 230) are available from Seed Savers Exchange (Decorah, Iowa), seedsavers.org, a nonprofit cooperative "keeping heirloom seeds where they belong: in our gardens and on our tables"; Irish Seed Savers Association (Capparoe, Ireland), irishseedsavers.ie, which maintains Ireland's only public seed bank plus the national collection of Irish heritage apple trees in order to "protect Ireland's food crop heritage for future generations"; and Brown Envelope Seeds (West Cork, Ireland), brownenvelopeseeds.com, a fine Irish company selling "organic vegetable, grain and herb seed grown on the farm in West Cork." Also see "The 10 Best Seed Companies for Heirloom and Non-GMO Seeds," by Dawn Gifford, Small Footprint Family website, smallfootprintfamily.com/the-10-best-seed-companies-for-heirloom-seeds.

Farming with nature (page 245) is exemplified by Alan Watson Featherstone, who founded Trees for Life, treesforlife.org.uk, with a vision of "a revitalised wild forest in the Highlands of Scotland, providing space for wildlife to flourish and communities to thrive"; and Rebecca Hosking, who has put forth eight principles of "agriwilding" on her website, rebeccahosking.co.uk.

Natural sewage treatment (page 248) is illustrated in "The Living Machine: An Ecological Approach to Poo," by Tafline Laylin, *Ecologist*, 8 June 2010, theecologist.org/2010/jun/08/living-machine-ecological-approach-poo. Instructions for building your own composting toilet can be found at humanurehandbook.com/instructions.html.

Native Plants

Douglas W. Tallamy, *Bringing Nature Home: How You Can Sustain Wildlife with Native Plants*, updated and expanded edition (Portland, OR: Timber Press, 2009).

——, *Nature's Best Hope: A New Approach to Conservation That Starts in Your Yard* (Portland, OR: Timber Press, 2019).

Douglas Tallamy's Hub: homegrownnationalpark.org/tallamys-hub-1. Contains new writing and interviews.

Great identification books on native plants are available now for everywhere in the world. Also, there are wonderful plant identification apps for phones if you like to work that way. I find these really helpful, though some of them are not dependable and you need a decent book as a backup.

These databases can also help with plant identification:

Ecological Flora of the British Isles, ecoflora.org.uk

Native plants database, New Zealand Department of Conservation website, doc.govt.nz/nature/native-plants/

Native Plants of North America database, Lady Bird Johnson Wildflower Center website, wildflower.org/plants-main

Online Atlas of the British and Irish Flora, brc.ac.uk/plantatlas/

Plant Database of the Australian Plants Society, resources.austplants.com.au/plant-database

PlantZAfrica, South African National Biodiversity Institute website, pza.sanbi.org

Larval Host Plants

Larval Host Plants for Butterflies and Moths, list on the EcoBeneficial! website, ecobeneficial.com/pvg/larval-host-plants-for-butterflies-and-moths/

Peter R. May, *Larval Foodplants of the Butterflies of Great Britain and Ireland* (London: Amateur Entomologists' Society, 2003).

Agroforestry, Regenerative Agriculture, and Permaculture

The website Permaculture Design with Delvin Solkinson and Grace Solkinson, permaculturedesign.earth, is a valuable resource where you can buy their wonderful book *Permaculture Design Notes*, a deeply knowledgeable offering from two permaculture visionaries.

Agroforestry Research Trust (UK), agroforestry.co.uk, is a research organization and plant nursery run by Martin Crawford, a leader in forest gardening. Offers forest garden plants and seeds, courses, seminars, and tours.

Jessie Bloom and Dave Boehnlein, *Practical Permaculture: For Home Landscapes, Your Community, and the Whole Earth* (Portland, OR: Timber Press, 2015).

Martin Crawford, *Creating a Forest Garden: Working with Nature to Grow Edible Crops* (Totnes, Devon, UK: Green Books, 2010).

Paul Hawken, *Regeneration: Ending the Climate Crisis in One Generation* (New York: Penguin, 2021).

Toby Hemenway, *Gaia's Garden: A Guide to Home-Scale Permaculture*, 2nd edition (White River Junction, VT: Chelsea Green, 2009).

Dave Jacke with Eric Toensmeier, *Edible Forest Gardens*, 2 volumes (White River Junction, VT: Chelsea Green, 2005).

Plants for a Future, *Plants for Your Food Forest: 500 Plants for Temperate Food Forests and Permaculture Gardens* (UK: Plants for a Future, 2021).

Eric Toensmeier, *Paradise Lot: Two Plant Geeks, One-Tenth of an Acre, and the Making of an Edible Garden Oasis in the City* (White River Junction, VT: Chelsea Green, 2013).

Indigenous Wisdom

Indigenous nonprofits that need support include Survival International, survivalinternational.org, which champions tribal peoples around the world, helping them defend their lives, protect their lands, and determine their own futures; Amazon Frontlines, amazonfrontlines.org, "Defending indigenous rights to land, life and cultural survival in the Amazon rainforest"; Minga Indigena, mingaindigena.org, "The traditional knowledge of Indigenous people at the service of humanity"; The Fountain Earth, thefountain.earth, "Sacred lands, sacred cultures, sacred economics"; and The Cultural Conservancy, nativeland.org, a Native-led organization based in the San Francisco Bay Area.

Robin Wall Kimmerer, *Braiding Sweetgrass: Indigenous Wisdom, Scientific Knowledge, and the Teachings of Plants* (Minneapolis, MN: Milkweed Editions, 2013).

Tyson Yunkaporta, *Sand Talk: How Indigenous Thinking Can Save the World* (New York: HarperOne, 2020).

Acknowledgments

Thank you to Claire Leadbitter and Ruth Evans. Your support and creativity are the foundation of all of this.

Thanks to Moya McGinley, Fran Mills, Sèan Bergin, and Clare Meleady Smith, who freely give your time and knowledge and good humour to run the We Are the ARK group online.

Also thank you to Julia Jackson of Grounded, Patricia Van Note, Paul Reynolds, Joseph Doyle, Jenn Halter Prenda, Brian McClintic of Viticole Wine, and Frances Gallagher of Rinn Bearna Aquatics for your knowledge, reading, and constant support.

To James Munnelly, Eileen Kelliher, and Pat O'Sullivan-Greene, thank you for your time, belief, and friendship.

Many thanks are due to Timber Press for believing in my book and to Lorraine Anderson for your gentle hand and patience with me in the edit.

Finally, a huge thank you to all the wonderful ARKevists out there across the globe who are powering ahead and changing the world patch by patch. I'm grateful to every single one of you for your good natures and generous spirits.

Index

Claire Leadbitter

Mary Reynolds is a reformed, internationally acclaimed landscape designer. In 2002 as a complete unknown she won a gold medal for her garden design at the Royal Horticultural Society's Chelsea Flower Show in London, the story of which was made into the 2016 movie *Dare to Be Wild*. Best-selling author of *The Garden Awakening*, Mary is a motivational speaker and founder of the global movement We Are the ARK. She's a single mum who likes to campaign against evil multinational efforts to kill off everything with pesticides, herbicides, GMOs, and fossil fuel craziness, all while she grows and guides her ARK, two almost-cooked boy and girl monsters, and a neurotic dog, with as much grace and love as possible.